1968

This book may be kept

FOURTEEN DAYS

A fine will b

DIRECTIONS IN MODERN POETRY

Books by Elizabeth Drew

DIRECTIONS IN MODERN POETRY
(in Collaboration with John L. Sweeney)

DISCOVERING DRAMA

DISCOVERING POETRY

THE ENJOYMENT OF LITERATURE

Directions in
MODERN
POETRY

➤➤ ➤➤ ➤➤ ➤➤ ➤➤ ➤➤ ➤➤ ➤➤ ➤➤ ➤➤ ◄◄ ◄◄ ◄◄ ◄◄ ◄◄ ◄◄ ◄◄ ◄◄ ◄◄ ◄◄

by ELIZABETH DREW

in Collaboration with
JOHN L. SWEENEY

"Years of the Modern! Propulsions
toward what capes?"
Hart Crane.

GORDIAN PRESS
New York
1967

Originally Published 1940
Reprinted 1967

Published by GORDIAN PRESS with the
Permission of W. W. Norton, Inc.

For

P. M. Sweeney

⇛ ⇛ ⇛ CONTENTS ⇚ ⇚ ⇚

⋙ ⋙ ⋙ ACKNOWLEDGMENTS ⋘ ⋘ ⋘

For permission to use selections the authors are indebted to the following:

The Macmillan Company for W. B. Yeats' *The Scholars, Leda and the Swan, Byzantium.*

The Viking Press, Inc., for D. H. Lawrence's *Flowers and Men.*

Harcourt, Brace & Company and T. S. Eliot for the extracts from the poetry of T. S. Eliot.

Farrar and Rinehart, Inc., and Ezra Pound for the extracts from the *Cantos.*

Alfred A. Knopf, Inc., and Wallace Stevens for *The Emperor of Ice-Cream* from *Harmonium.*

Alfred A. Knopf, Inc., and John Crowe Ransom for *The Equilibrists* from *Two Gentlemen in Bonds.*

Liveright Publishing Corporation for *Voyages II* from *Collected Poems of Hart Crane.*

New Directions and William Carlos Williams for *Red Wheel Barrow.*

Harper & Brothers and Edna St. Vincent Millay for *Euclid Alone Has Looked on Beauty Bare.*

Faber & Faber, Ltd., and Roy Campbell for *The Zebras.*

Chatto and Windus and William Empson for *Legal Fiction* and *Note on Local Flora.*

Oxford University Press and Richard Eberhart for *To a Lamb* from *Reading the Spirit.*

Random House, Inc., and W. H. Auden for *Sir, No Man's Enemy* and *Voltaire at Ferney*.

The *New Statesman* and *Nation* and Louis MacNeice for *Les Sylphides*.

The *New Masses* and James Agee for *Sunday: Outskirts of Knoxville, Tenn.*

W. W. Norton and Company, Inc., and Robert Fitzgerald for *Portrait*.

TO write of the past is very much easier than to write of the present. Time gives proportion and perspective, and ignorance supplies a frame which limits and focuses our vision. The critical faculty, too, can prop itself on tradition and the tried judgment of the years. The poetry we receive from the past has been sifted through the mesh of time and the grain separated from the chaff, the permanent from the ephemeral. In judging contemporary verse, the task of time must be performed by the individual critic; the critic's mind and taste must play the part of the sieve of the ages, the critic's unaided ear must recognize the 'powerful rhyme' which carries the authentic note of immortality.

T. S. Eliot has said that to select a good new poem, to respond properly to a new poetic situation, is the most severe test of a critic. It is easy to illustrate its severity from the past history of criticism. We all know the welcome which Wordsworth and, later, Keats received at the hands of the reviewers. We can come even nearer home than that. Reviewing *The Waste Land* in *The London Mercury* in 1923, J. C. Squire (now Sir John Squire) wrote: 'Conceivably, what is attempted here . . . is a faithful transcript of the poet's wandering thoughts when in a state of erudite depression. A grunt would serve equally well.' And later (1926): 'The kindest thing one can suppose is that he is experimenting with automatic writing. Why on earth he bothers to write at all it is difficult to conceive.' And this was not the opinion of a desiccated academic, but the editorial verdict of a man of Eliot's own generation.

In spite of the difficulty of contemporary appraisal, however, there is no other poetry which can have quite the same interest for us as the poetry of our own day; the poetry whose material is the life about us here and now, of which we are a living part; the poetry whose creators are alive in the way we ourselves are alive, who have to meet life on the same terms as we meet it; the poetry which is written for *us*. For a poet does not consciously address posterity, he writes to fellow men and women in his own age. At all times, poetry has revealed man to himself, in his unchanging essence, but we turn to the poet of our own day to make us aware not only of the changeless nature of the human heart, but of the pulse of the present. We ask him to reveal and clarify our life by showing it to us through a vision different from ours and deeper. We ask him to organize the conflicting welter of impressions which is the actual process of living, into the ordered and disciplined integrations of experience which are works of art.

The reader who really cares about poetry—the reader who is prepared to make some effort to receive what poetry can give—asks this. For, as Wordsworth says, genius represents an advance or a conquest made by the soul of the poet in the sphere of human sensibility, and it is not to be supposed that the reader can share in that conquest by following 'like an Indian prince or general—stretched on his palanquin, and borne by his slaves. No, he is invigorated and inspirited by his leader, in order that he may exert himself; for he cannot proceed in quiescence, he cannot be carried like a dead weight.'

It is for the active reader that this book is written. It does not aim at being a chatty review of those poets who are most in the public eye, for the evolution of poetry is never that of the survival of the slickest. Nor does it pretend to be objective, unprejudiced and impartial. Poor Ophelia's wits were crazed when she went around handing out flowers to everyone without discrimination. 'You need not be afraid,' said Elizabeth to Jane Bennett in *Pride and Prejudice*, 'that I shall encroach on *your* privilege of universal goodwill'—and indeed the Jane Bennetts in criticism as in life are inclined to be slightly insipid. It is impossible to have a lively interest in poetry and not to have strong personal feelings about it; and in the end every reader must own that though he may try to be detached, his criticism is bound to be the result of his own individual taste. Nor can such a book as this hope to be inclusive. Like the Irishman's evidence, it is chock full of omissions. There is a considerable quantity of minor verse written today, and much of it is pleasing, graceful, genuine and workmanlike. But such verse needs no criticism to interpret it, and this is primarily a book of interpretation. Our aim is to try to give some account of the variety and significance of the poetry of the last twenty-five years, and particularly to do so by the method of supporting our generalizations by example and examination.

Contemporary poetry is often difficult poetry. The reasons for this are examined in the book, but even when the reasons are understood, the poetry remains difficult. The authors agree with C. Day Lewis that one of the duties of a critic is 'to erect signposts for the reader, to help him over difficult places, and to make him feel that the journey is worth undertaking.' There are other critics who disapprove of this method, who hold that the only way to come at the spirit of poetry is by direct intuition; that 'we murder to dissect.' Ways of reading, like the enjoyment of the thing read, must finally be matters of personal choice, but it is difficult to see how a good poem can lose anything by elucidation. The value of analysis is that it makes possible a *fuller* experience of the poem; for, by examining a poem in the light of paraphrase, the 'poetic process' is sometimes clarified, revealing the sources of the poet's power and the particular uses of language which distinguish his art from that of prose.

It is impossible, however, to discuss contemporary poetry in general without some discussion of the contemporary world. Man's conquest of matter and the emergence of a huge industrial and scientific civilization have transformed our world—which is also the poet's world. The source of Sir John Squire's failure in his criticism of Eliot was not only an insensitiveness to new rhythmic word patterns but also the fact that 'any radical change in poetic form is likely to be a symptom of some very much deeper change in society and the individual.' These changes are not at the moment a cheering subject, and are not of a kind to nourish or stimulate a flourishing

literary culture. What they are, and their apparent effect
on the individual poets who have been living through
them, we shall try to investigate in the first part of the
book. The subject of the second part is the poet as artist,
as a worker in a particular medium through which his
effects must be gained. Here again, there is a great deal of
gloomy wagging of heads. Conservative critics complain
that the modern poet is an iconoclast, a mere vandal of
tradition; they see him as a tennis player who has set out
to play tennis and decides that the lines of the court are
cramping to his liberty, that the net is in the way and had
better be abolished, and that the racket is a poor instrument anyway and should be superseded. But they forget
that the rules of tennis were imposed by people who
played an older game, and changed and modified it into
its present form, and that other people evolved other
varieties of games also played with a ball, and kicked it
over a bar, or coaxed it into a hole with a club, or hit
it with a bat and ran. The success of poetry can be judged
only by its power to reveal and enlarge and intensify
all kinds of human experience. If it accomplish this, it does
not matter what rules it breaks or what means it uses.

Poetry is both an impulse and a discipline. To appreciate
it fully the reader must know and feel its matter and its
manner. The first essential is to possess a warm and lively
interest in human experience. Cold scholarship, as Yeats
knew, is not enough.

> Bald heads forgetful of their sins,
> Old, learned, respectable bald heads
> Edit and annotate the lines
> That young men, tossing on their beds,

Rhymed out in love's despair
To flatter beauty's ignorant ear.

All shuffle there; all cough in ink;
All wear the carpet with their shoes;
All think what other people think;
All know the man their neighbour knows.
Lord, what would they say
Did their Catullus walk that way?

Poets are first and foremost human beings. We must keep ourselves alive to more than the printed word. But neither is the 'ignorant ear' enough. For poets are artists as well as human beings; and as Gerard Manley Hopkins wrote:

Some men exercise a deep influence on their own age in virtue of certain powers at that time original, new and stimulating, which afterwards ceasing to stimulate their fame declines; because it was not supported by an execution, an achievement equal to the power. For nothing but fine execution survives long.

PART I. *The Substance of Poetry*

CHAPTER 1

The Poet and His Audience

. . . the Public; a thing I cannot help looking upon
as an Enemy, and which I cannot address without
feelings of Hostility.
   I never wrote one single Line of Poetry with the
least Shadow of public thought.
                    JOHN KEATS. Letter to John Ham-
                         ilton Reynolds. April 1818

ART is a natural function of man. It is inherent in
his nature, as one of his means of communication
with his fellows—

Art is a human activity consisting in this, that one man
consciously, by means of certain external signs, hands on
to others feelings he has lived through, and that others
are infected by those feelings and also experience them.

Tolstoi's definition is a simple one, but it is comprehensive.
Poetry is a means of human communication: the poet is
a man speaking to men. The Hebrew prophets and the
troubadours, the author of *Beowulf* and Baudelaire,
Aeschylus and Auden are all part of the same basic
human exercise. All down the ages there have been men
whose nature urges them to transmit their experience of
life in words; to be articulate where others are satisfied to
remain silent. These are the poets—the men who have
striven eagerly and passionately to find 'the best words
in the best order' to make that experience live again.

   The poet is a spokesman among his fellows. This does

not mean that he is another variety of preacher or political leader, delivering a 'message' or outlining a policy or dogma. A poem has a living reality of its own: it is not religion or ethics or philosophy or sociology. The poet does not work upon his listeners by providing beliefs or moral codes for them, or by outlining political, philosophical or economic systems. All these things *may* enter into poetry; but the poet is concerned with them only in so far as they can be related to his personal vision of human experience. The poet's domain is the life of Man and the lives of men in their actions, thoughts and emotions, interpreted through the power of words. And readers and listeners of all ages have acclaimed poets, not because in them they have found their human problems solved, but because through them they have found their capacities for living enriched and enlarged and their understanding deepened. 'No man can read Hardy's poems but that his own life, and forgotten moments of it, will come back to him, a flash here and an hour there. Have you a better test of true poetry?' says Ezra Pound in his book on Culture. But such a test restricts the experience of poetry to very limited ground. It is not only memory and recognition which are stirred, but new powers of living are developed, and fresh areas of sensibility uncovered. Poetry is not 'like life,' but it awakens and quickens life in us. Human lovers do not speak like Romeo and Juliet, but they feel that Shakespeare has in them revealed the experiences and sensations of being in love in all their fullness and intensity. The poet has found adequate expression for all that they themselves dimly and dumbly feel. His words bring to the surface of the listener's consciousness physical and mental and spiritual experiences which otherwise would lie sleeping, inert and cloddish.

The poet is simply a man like other men, but with a greater power of living *into* experience, of piercing to its core, of widening it by memory and association, of sharpening it by acute sensibility. He communicates this through the medium of words, and it follows that any fully conscious enjoyment of poetry raises two questions. First, what is the quality, the width, the depth, the coloring and composition of the mind which possesses this experiencing power? Second, how does he make this known to us? By the first question we mean, how does the poet feel, see and think about life? To what aspects of living is he particularly sensitive? Is he, like Wordsworth or Blake, a prophet, a seer, who feels the external world to be a symbol only of some larger spiritual reality; or is he, like Chaucer or Browning, excited mainly by stories of the personal relationships of human beings as they live their lives; or is he absorbed in the psychological processes of the individual human being, like Donne or Eliot; or is his main interest in an intellectual judgment of society, as in Dryden or Pope; or in romantic and sensuous experience, as in Keats or Rossetti; or in graceful, harmonious simplicity, as in Herrick; or in moral value, as in Arnold? We ask, what is the human significance and span and depth of the poet; what is the *substance* of his poetry? Our second question includes further queries. What do we mean by 'imagination'; how does the quality of the poet's mind and vision reveal itself to us, and infect us with his own consciousness of living? What is the poetic *process* by which experience is converted into eloquence and communication?

We shall see later that these two aspects of poetry are ultimately inseparable; we become aware of the poet's experience only through the poetic process. But the average reader of poetry finds no difficulty in making a distinction in his mind. He knows that he takes active pleasure in poetic artistry: in formal pattern, rhythm, melody, image-making, the quality of words. If he has any interest in the mysteries behind creation, he loves to explore the sources of that pleasure. But he knows too that it is its power of amplifying and stimulating his sense of *living* which is its great human value. He knows that the editorial in the newspaper may say, '*We may unhesitatingly assert that we shall not relax our efforts nor cease to struggle in this great conflict for human happiness and moral welfare until our objectives have clearly been obtained,*' and that it does not move him, but that when it has been translated by the poetic process it kindles and wakens and challenges his whole nature.

> Bring me my Bow of burning gold!
> Bring me my Arrows of desire!
> Bring me my Spear! O clouds, unfold!
> Bring me my chariot of fire!
>
> I shall not cease from mental fight
> Nor shall my Sword sleep in my hand,
> Till we have built Jerusalem
> In England's green and pleasant land.

It is first and foremost the *spirit* of the poet that he hears and feels in the vivid associations of Blake's imagery.

The spirit of the poet, like that of all other men, is conditioned by two forces, personality and environment. Rousseau said we must choose either to be individuals or to be members of a community; but we must be both, we have no choice. The poet is an individual, possessing a certain physical, mental and emotional constitution which makes him unique just as every human creature is unique. He is intensely conscious of this. One of the impulses behind his writing of poetry is not only to interpret experience to others but to clarify and objectify it to himself, to incarnate his consciousness in a verbal pattern which shall give, as it were, another body to his own spirit. But his own spirit does not function in a vacuum, but in an environment. Whitman's 'O Me! O Life!' is every poet's motto, and 'life' means that he is alive at a particular epoch of the world's history, and in particular religious, political, social and cultural surroundings. The influence of these is pervasive and inescapable. As Eliot says, 'At the moment when one writes, one is what one is, and the damage of a lifetime, and the having been born into an unsettled society, cannot be repaired at the moment of composition.' A poet may be in sympathy with his environment or in revolt from it; he may accept it, or attack it, or attempt to elude it; but the very fact that he is alive and functions in it is a proof that he is on *some* sort of terms with it. What those terms are will be either implicit or explicit in his poetry.

§

But the position which the poet has held in the community of which he is a member has been modified profoundly during the course of history. In the drama and epic of the ancient world, poetry was at the heart of both the religion and the entertainment of the people, and the poet, therefore, was the life-giver to both. The bard, 'the skop,' the wandering minstrel and the ballad-singer carried on the tradition of poetic storytelling among the people, and as long as the religious drama lasted, poetry remained a part of the general religious life of the community. But during the last four hundred years cultural and economic changes have revolutionized the position of the poet. Gradually he lost touch with the general life of the community as a whole: he became detached, a member of a specialized group called 'men of letters,' and his influence shrank to the reading public, a small minority. For many generations, however, men of letters continued to play perhaps a major part in creating the culture of their day. They tended to be groups actively concerned with national and social ideas as well as with artistic ones. They deepened the reality and spread the scope of the fundamental values held by the intelligent society for which they wrote. In theater, salon, coffeehouse, club or academy of letters, literature retained its character as a public cultivated interest and amusement: the poet functioned in a social framework (although an increasingly limited one), and still possessed the strength which comes from participation in a positive communal outlook.

But while the value of a positive communal outlook cannot be overemphasized in a social culture, its importance for the individual poet can be, and is, very much overemphasized among the young poets of today. The history of literature proves that poetry has gained as much, or more, from poets who have set up an autonomy in their own kingdom, as from those who have enjoyed the cosier comfort which is drawn from a sense of a united standard of value. When a modern critic bemoans that 'when the artist lost contact with the people, something vital went out of his art,' he forgets that something equally vital might also come into it. The great poet as often as not has been a deliberate rebel from the social consciousness of his own age. Marlowe, Donne, Blake, Wordsworth, Baudelaire, Rimbaud, Hardy, Yeats, are examples. The poetry of some of these aided in the creation of a new social culture, while that of others revolutionized man's realization of himself, but none of them had a communal consciousness as a solid basis for his creative function. Thus when Herbert Read declares, 'It is almost impossible to be a poet in an industrial age,' or Edmund Wilson says 'The conditions which give rise to great literature are the phenomenon of highly developed literary technique in the hands of any writer who derives strength from a set of strongly established institutions,' or Auden states 'It is impossible that any artist can do his best except in a community united in sympathy, sense of worth and aspiration,' the facts are against them. Every poet would no doubt enjoy a totalitarian public of his own way of thinking, but poetry can spring as strongly out of resistance as from acceptance, and the doctrine of the congenial period will not bear scrutiny. All the modern talk of the incapacity of the artist to function in this, that or the other social and economic environment can be disproved by any study of the past. Poetry has been written under monarchies, democracies and dictatorships, in times of religious and political persecution, in war and in peace; it has been written by peasants and by princes, by scholars and scamps, by hermits and cosmopolitans, by revolutionaries and by quietists, by priests, by rationalists and by madmen. It is much tougher than its timorous critics realize, but whenever its lifeblood becomes slightly anaemic there are always a mournful company who hover over what they are sure is its deathbed—like a panicky young mother convinced that her first-born is in convulsions when it is only suffering from colic.

§

But to point this out is not to deny that it is obviously *easier* to write well in a community dominated by a common cultural outlook with which the poet is in sympathy, and that communities in which poetry has performed its richest social service have always been of this character—societies such as that of Athens in the fifth century B. C., or that of Elizabethan England. For the kinship or antipathy which exists between the poet and his audience frequently modifies the use, as it were, he can make of his own personality. We all know from experience how differently our own individual consciousness reacts to a sympathetic, a stimulating, a hostile or an indifferent audience, and exactly the same thing applies to the relationship of the poet and the community in which he works. Indeed, the fact that the artist possesses a sensibility beyond the average makes him peculiarly impressionable to his environment and the temper of his times. The great poet, as we have seen, can dominate any environment. If he can consort in a vital sympathy with the faith and culture of his own day, he swims triumphantly on the

crest of the whole tide of his time, like Shakespeare or
Pope; but equally he can achieve fullness of living by a
conscious revolt from the age in which he is writing, by
challenging it and defying it in the strength of his own
individual values, like Wordsworth or Whitman. The
poets of less dynamic temperament cannot achieve this.
There are always the happy few who can content themselves in a congenial isolation: poets such as the seventeenth century religious lyrists, or Blake or Emily Dickinson or Hardy. But there are many who are defeated by
their environment if they are out of sympathy with it.
Thus we feel that poets such as Collins in the eighteenth
century, or Clough in the nineteenth, or Roy Campbell
in the twentieth, failed to realize themselves fully because
the spirit of their age was alien to that of their own genius
and thwarted it, while they had not the poetic or individual stature to make poetry out of their resistance.
We feel the same about Tennyson, whose real nature,
apart from his delicate sensuous perceptions, was sardonic
and introspective, and who achieved the contemporary
success of his later years by deliberately giving the Victorian public what it liked, while he stultified his true
gifts and his future fame by doing so. He gained the
world and lost his own soul. Hopkins, at the other extreme, kept his own spirit and his poetic genius unspotted,
but at the cost of an almost absolute loneliness of purpose
which is the hardest fate of all for a poet to bear, since
it is of the very nature of his art to communicate with
his fellows. And it is significant, in view of Hopkins' own
obscurity and of the character of much modern poetry,
that Hopkins wrote in a letter to Bridges, 'To return to

composition for a moment: what I want there, to be more
intelligible, smooth, and less singular, is an audience.'

§

It is this same loneliness which is tormenting the poets
of our own age—and justly. For there has certainly never
been an age when poetry has been so completely divorced
from national and communal life as it has been for the
last twenty years. It is true that throughout its history it
has been very much more closely knit into the general
cultural and social fabric in some ages than in others. Indeed, there seems to be a kind of ebb and flow in the
matter, so that in one age the general coloring of poetry
will be social and in the next individualistic. The great
Elizabethan age, when every class and calling seems to
have responded, at some level, to the poetic drama, was
followed by the seventeenth century, the great age of
the lyric, of lyrics singing of love and religion, the two
great private and personal rhythms of the human spirit;
while the fine flower of the contemporary Puritan culture
blossomed in the most lonely of all great poets, Milton.
Then came the eighteenth century, with its emphasis on
political and social interests, and that in turn was followed by the romantic revival, with its awakening to individual spiritual values. Again in the Victorian age we
find a 'social' poetry, with its insistence on the corporate
elements in human existence, on conduct and social moral-
ity. It is the fashion nowadays to belittle Victorian culture, but at no time since the Elizabethan age has poetry
been so much a part of the life of the community as it
was then. We laugh at the minor verse of that age today,

and we do right to despise most of it if we are speaking in terms of literary criticism, but if we are speaking in terms of a social culture the position is very different. For at least the Victorians of all classes were familiar with a communal poetry which told of the simple moral values by which simple people in all ages live their lives. In homes and schools, at the church social and the penny reading, in the recitation and the sermon, verse colored their lives, and the examples of Casabianca and the hero of *Excelsior*, of Sir Richard Grenville and the Minstrel Boy, joined the company of Sir Patrick Spens and Robin Hood and Bonnie Prince Charlie in the popular imagination.

The picture today is certainly very different. Why is it that in fifty years or so there has been such a complete cultural change?

§

In the answer is involved the whole character of our contemporary civilization. For as Ezra Pound says, 'When something is wrong with the arts it is not wrong with the arts *only*.' Wordsworth, with the uncanny vision of genius, foretold in his Preface to the *Lyrical Ballads* in 1800 the direction in which everything was heading:

For a multitude of causes, unknown to former times, are now acting with a combined force to blunt the discriminating powers of the mind, and unfitting it for all voluntary exertion, to reduce it to a state of almost savage torpor. The most effective of these causes are the great national events which are daily taking place, and the increasing accumulation of men in cities, where the uniformity of their occupations produces a craving for ex-

traordinary incident, which the rapid communication of
intelligence hourly gratifies.

In the hundred and forty years since this was written
every factor in the situation has tightened its grip on
the traditional cultural standards. Political, economic and
class struggles have disintegrated the old homogeneous
nineteenth century society, producing everywhere a profound awareness of insecurity and instability. At the same
time, undreamed-of advances in scientific and technical
achievement have steadily encroached upon every area
of work and play. Progress has been measured everywhere by mechanical and materialistic standards. In in-
dustry 'the ritual of the endless belt, the sequence of cog
and tooth' has everywhere replaced the rhythmic creation
of man's own hands.

> Robot to west of us, puppet to east of us,
> Magnetic clutches rotating counterwise
> Govern our gearing . . .
> Caps off to Arkwright and Ford! *

In amusement, the same forces have operated and the
same standards hold good; so that now not only the vast
multitude of what we might call the Ignorantia, but also
large sections of the so-called Intelligentsia, are exposed
perpetually to the hypnotic appeal of the motion picture,
the radio and the popular press—amusements which, instead of stimulating their spiritual and mental faculties,
and opening their eyes and ears to invigorating experience,
seem rather to conspire to suffocate their intelligence and
to sap their energy of mind by providing merely *passive*

* Ronald Bottrall.

diversion to which they need bring no active co-operation whatever.

The result of all this has been to create not so much a hostility, as a vast and increasing indifference and in-attention to cultural values among the vast majority of the population, emerging in a sharp and deep cleavage between the many, to whom literature means some variety of journalism, good or bad, some form of information or amusement, and the few, to whom it means art.

In any age, it is of course always upon a very small minority that the discerning and critically conscious ap-preciation of literary art depends. But this is of no con-sequence if the finer sensibilities of the race, embodied in its artists, are in relation with a real cultural tradition shared by the people at large. We do not suppose that the Elizabethan audience noted the very subtle imagery of disease and decay which runs through *Hamlet*, giving the whole play a particular flavor to those sensitive to the overtones of poetry; but that in no way impaired their realization that Shakespeare was speaking to them in a language of action, character and words—a language of human and intellectual values—which, fundamentally, they shared with him.

Poets in all ages have possessed a finer consciousness than that of the ordinary man. But in earlier days the emphasis fell on the amount poets possessed *in common with* the ordinary man. The basis of their communication was the intellectual and emotional experience of the com-munity, *plus* the values of revelation and interpretation which their own finer powers made possible. Now it is the degree of consciousness which the poet possesses *in excess of* the ordinary man on which the emphasis falls, and which he aims to communicate. The great nineteenth century writers were the last who appealed to all social grades, who could feel that they were addressing a homogeneous society which shared the cultural tradition of which they were themselves the literary embodiment, and to whom they could speak in the language of common human experience.

§

Bad feelings on both sides have hardened the divorce between poetry and the reading public, so that while one side declares justly that never has there been a public with such execrable taste and blank ignorance about poetry, the other side retorts equally justly that never have poets taken less pains to satisfy the human needs of their readers, or been ruder about their readers' shortcomings. Ezra Pound in *Tenzone*, one of his early poems, asks the question, will people accept his songs? No, he answers, they will not, and he likens the multitude to a 'timorous wench' fleeing, howling with terror, from the advances of a centaur or a centurion. No, 'their virgin stupidity is untemptable.'

> I beg you, my friendly critics,
> Do not set about to procure me an audience.
> I mate with my free kind upon the crags. . . .

Now this attitude has an obvious danger. 'To believe that your impression holds good for others is to be released from the cramp and confinement of personality,' says Virginia Woolf; and the result of the conviction of the poet that he has nothing to say to the community at large has been that the material of poetry has been sought more and more in that cramped and confined territory. In rebellion against the quality of the society around him, feeling all its spiritual disorganization and communal dislocation, the poet withdrew into the only world in which he could feel sure of himself, the world of his art. Here he made his awareness of his own individuality the substance of his poetry, and his expression of that his sole contribution to the cultural content of the community. Poets tended to be mainly the same *type* of personality: the type who feels with abnormal acuteness, but feels *narrowly;* who experiences life intensely rather than profoundly or comprehensively; whose nervous system is more developed than his common human emotions, and who feels himself a rebel from, and at the same time superior to, the common social standards.

Meanwhile, the increased specialization in every branch of occupation, which is another symptom of the modern world, cut the poet off not only from the life of the general community, but even from his intellectual equals in other fields. His audience became a narrow literary coterie, or a set of different coteries, out of all contact with the solid body of contemporary cultivated society; so that it sometimes appears as if his relations with his fellow men are limited to fulsome praise of the members of his own group, and embittered attacks upon members of other groups. Instead of the poet being a man talking to men, or even a member of the intelligentsia talking to other members of the intelligentsia, he became an artist talking to other artists, or an artist talking to himself.

Instead of some recognized literary center, representing more or less widely the cultivated interests of the community—the court, the theater, the salon, the coffeehouse, the club, the houses of wealthy patrons—the only center of discussion becomes the studio. And when artists meet in studios in the company of other artists, they always do the same thing. They gossip; and they become impassioned, not about common human values, but about artistic values: they talk shop. With the result that the supreme interest of literature in the last twenty years has been in experimental technique. When this happens, it means that poetry has become *rootless*, for the roots of poetry are in life, not in craft.

Auden, in his *Letter to Lord Byron*, has given us a picture of the position.

> Art, if it doesn't start there, at least ends,
>   Whether aesthetics like the thought or not,
> In an attempt to entertain our friends;
>   And our first problem is to realise what
>   Peculiar friends the modern artist's got;
> It's possible a little dose of history
> May help us in unravelling this mystery.
>
>   . . . .
>
> We find two arts in the Augustan age:
>   One quick and graceful, and by no means holy
> Relying on his lordship's patronage;
>   The other pious, sober, moving slowly,
>   Appealing mainly to the poor and lowly.
> So Isaac Watts and Pope, each forced his entry
> To lower middle class and landed gentry.
>
>   . . . .
>
> The important point to notice, though, is this:
>   Each poet knew for whom he had to write,

Because their life was still the same as his.
    As long as art remained a parasite,
    On any class of persons it's alright;
The only thing it must be is attendant,
The only thing it mustn't, independent.

But artists though are human; and for man
    To be a scivvy is not nice at all:
So everyone will do the best he can
    To get a patch of ground which he can call
    His own. He doesn't really care how small
So long as he can style himself the master:
Unluckily for art, it's a disaster.

                .   .   .   .

Until the great Industrial Revolution
    The artist had to earn his livelihood:
However much he hated the intrusion
    Of patron's taste or public's fickle mood,
    He had to please or go without his food;
He had to keep his technique to himself
Or find no joint upon the larder shelf.

                .   .   .   .

So started what I call the Poet's Party:
    (Most of the guests were painters, never mind)—
The first few hours the atmosphere was hearty,
    With fireworks, fun, and games of every kind;
    All were enjoying it, no one was blind;
Brilliant the speeches improvised, the dances,
And brilliant, too, the technical advances.

                .   .   .   .

Today, alas, that happy crowded floor
    Looks very different: many are in tears:
Some have retired to bed and locked the door;
    And some swing madly from the chandeliers;
    Some have passed out entirely in the rears;
Some have been sick in corners; the sobering few
Are trying hard to think of something new.

Let us see then, what quality of work the Poet's Party produced, and what those are doing who are trying hard to think of something new.

CHAPTER 2

The Waste Land

What are the roots that clutch, what branches grow
Out of this stony rubbish?
                    T. S. ELIOT. *The Waste Land*

You are as good as a chorus, my lord. . . .
                    SHAKESPEARE. *Hamlet*

POETRY is not written by 'movements,' it is written by men. When we generalize about 'the spirit of the age' we sometimes forget that there are all varieties of temperaments alive in every age. We are inclined to think of the Victorian age as full of energy and optimism, with the air charged with moral ozone. Yet Matthew Arnold's lines

>   this strange disease of modern life,
> With its sick hurry, its divided aims . . .

might be by any of the young 'postwar' poets describing the contemporary world. Or compare these two passages:

Yes, society was diseased then, still it had some sound life left in it. But now the entire organism is dissolving and falling asunder. All the parts are refusing to perform their functions. . . .

Happy those run over in the street today, or drowned at sea. . . . They cannot be made a party to the general fiasco. For of that growth which in maturity had seemed eternal it is now no tint of thought or feeling that has tarnished, but the great ordered flower itself is withering: its life-blood dwindled to an unimportant trickle.

The former is from Mallock's *The New Republic*, published in 1877, the latter from Auden and Isherwood's *The Ascent of F6*, sixty years later; one written in what is commonly considered an age of faith, the other in an age of disillusion. The remarks prove nothing, except that, as another character in *The New Republic* remarks: 'Many thoughtful people think that there is more that is bad in the present than there has ever been in the past. Many thoughtful people in all ages have thought the same.' It is obvious that such an attitude is the product of an individual temperament, not a broad reflection of the society itself. In the same way *we* regard the age of Pericles as a 'golden age' of man, yet in that very period Sophocles contended that man's best fate was never to have been born.

In spite of all this, there is some basis for talking about the spirit of an age. Physical, moral, emotional, intellectual, artistic, political and social forces interpenetrate and interblend in different proportions to form varying cultural climates, and the poet finds himself born into, and breathing, a time-ether which pervades and permeates his whole temporal environment. The fact that he possesses an abnormally acute sensibility makes him peculiarly impressionable to this environment. For him certain channels of intellectual and emotional development will be easily accessible and others will be blocked. According to his own temperament he will find himself sympathetic or antipathetic to the time-spirit. If he is antipathetic to it, he will, according to his degree of genius, either fulfill his own spirit in an expression of an individual vision, or find his own nature frustrated by his necessary isolation. 'The transaction between a writer and the spirit of the age is one of infinite delicacy,' as Virginia Woolf says, 'and upon a nice arrangement between the two the whole future of his work depends.'

§

There were many reasons why the whole character of the twentieth century should be very different from that of the nineteenth. The great wave of vitality and national expansions which, during the Victorian period, swept both England and America to a high-water mark of material prosperity, left in its ebb a highly developed industrial civilization and a clear path for all the currents of scientific and mechanistic thought which were to flood the new century. But literature, which had been nourished by the general vigor of the time, and not at all by the practical interests of the period, declined as the spirit itself dispersed. Before the end of the century that positive, homogeneous, energetic social culture which collaborated with the great Victorian writers had disintegrated.

> Be hate that fruit or love that fruit
> It forwards the general deed of man,
> And each of the many helps to recruit
> The life of the race by a general plan,
> Each living his own to boot.

Browning, booming out his hearty, glib optimism, had been followed by Hardy, while the literary coterie of the nineties already marked the arrival of an entirely new idea. Art had begun to be created for Art's sake. The great age of groups and 'movements' began. The eighteenth century poets did not call themselves classicists, nor the nineteenth century poets call themselves romanticists; their poetic coloring was simply the quality of their whole response to the whole of life. But the literary history of the late nineteenth century ànd early twentieth is full of theories and isms—Symbolism, Futurism, Imagism, Vorticism, Expressionism, Dadaism, Surrealism—which provided artistic creeds for artist groups, and set the individual artist apart from the community in the popular opinion.

It was only one of these, Symbolism, which had any notable effect upon the course of poetry in England and America, but it was directly from the French Symbolists of the late nineteenth century that the leading poet of the postwar period drew his inspiration.

The publication of *The Waste Land* in 1922 will probably remain the outstanding literary landmark of our period. Like the *Lyrical Ballads* of a hundred and twenty years earlier, it will stand as the outward symbol of the arrival of a completely new orientation towards human experience and towards its expression in language. Many of the ideas behind this new type of poetry were not new. Rimbaud, Verlaine and Mallarmé had all insisted that the only reality in life was the inner reality, that the world in which the poet lived transcended the world of common experience; they taught years earlier that the appeal of poetry should never be to the logic of the intelligence, but to the logic of the imagination—that its method should not be one of direct statement or description, but one of oblique image and suggestion. Eliot, however, was mainly influenced by Laforgue, whose flavor is different from that of the early Symbolists. Eliot's early

poems have the same underlying theme as Laforgue's—
the damage to human values caused by the invasion of
an industrial civilization. They create Laforguian characters such as Mr. Prufrock and the hero of *Portrait of
a Lady*, self-conscious misfits in a conventional bourgeoisie, who are aware not only of its humbug, but of
their own inadequacy to dominate it. And Eliot, like Laforgue, developed a method of composition which presented his material in a medley of direct drama and associative imagery.

Between the age in which Laforgue wrote and the appearance of *The Waste Land* two influences were at work
which inevitably colored both the matter and the manner
of Eliot's writing. First of all, the atmosphere engendered
by the Great War and its aftermath had proved a mood
of disillusionment, dismay and fear. This is illustrated by
the speech with which Valéry opened a conference at
Zurich in November 1922.*

The storm has died away, and still we are uneasy, as if
the storm were about to break. Almost all the affairs of
men remain in a terrible uncertainty. We think of what
has disappeared, we are almost destroyed by what has
been destroyed; we do not know what will be born, and
we fear the future not without reason. We hope vaguely,
we dread precisely; our fears are infinitely more precise
than our hopes; we confess that the charm of life is behind us, that abundance is behind but doubt and disorder
are in us and with us. There is no thinking man . . . who
can hope to dominate this anxiety, to escape from this
impression of darkness, to measure the probable duration
of this period when the vital relations of humanity are
disturbed profoundly.

* Published in *Variété*.

This might almost stand as an analysis of the atmosphere of *The Waste Land*. The other factor of which we are everywhere conscious in Eliot's early work (as in that of his great prose contemporary, James Joyce) is that research in psychoanalysis had enormously extended the technique for the study of the subconscious processes of the human mind.

§

'The poet,' in I. A. Richards' words, 'is the point at which the growth of the mind shows itself.' In Eliot's early poetry the whole cultural situation of the moment is given body and outline. In it we have the expression of the divorce between the community and its old cultural unity, between the poet and the people; we also feel the weariness and staleness of spirit which paralyze all positive attitudes, and the awareness of a new dimension in the apprehension of life through psychological investigation.

The theme of the whole of Eliot's *Poems 1909–1925* is the quality of the civilization, that 'smoky candle-end of time,' of which the poet finds himself a part, and the conviction that it is irretrievably doomed: 'the rats are underneath the piles.' In these poems, though there is no direct discussion of the subject, he creates symbol after symbol to point to the character of contemporary society, and to build up in the mind of the reader a series of powerful pictures and imaginative concepts giving the clue to his vision. *Gerontion*, published in 1920, shows his matter and manner best.

> Here I am, an old man in a dry month,
> Being read to by a boy, waiting for rain.

I was neither at the hot gates
Nor fought in the warm rain
Nor knee deep in the salt marsh, heaving a cutlass,
Bitten by flies, fought.
My house is a decayed house,
And the jew squats on the window sill, the owner,
Spawned in some estaminet of Antwerp,
Blistered in Brussels, patched and peeled in London.
The goat coughs at night in the field overhead;
Rocks, moss, stonecrop, iron, merds,
The woman keeps the kitchen, makes tea,
Sneezes at evening, poking the peevish gutter.
                              I an old man,
A dull head among windy spaces.

This was a startling kind of poetry for a public used to reading the mild Georgians or the slight and objective Imagists. It was dismissed as unintelligible by all but a few. To many it remains so still; and since the secret of enjoying much modern poetry lies in grasping what the poet is doing when he writes with this oblique and disguised approach to his theme, we might spend a moment analyzing this passage.

Gerontion, the old man, is himself a symbol of our dying civilization. He sits in a parched, unfertile land, listening perhaps to some tales of past greatness, and sees, in a series of pictures and images, what his life is. He has had no youth of active struggle for freedom on which he can look back proudly (the hot gates = Thermopylae): he is alive in a decayed world that belongs to a people more interested in money than in spiritual or cultural values. Even his lust is no longer natural and healthy. It is a world of hardness, torpor, barrenness, machinery, filth. The women are drudges, not real homemakers and mothers of children, but occupied with petty details of housekeeping and health; inefficient and sour. And he himself is old, stupid, directionless.*

Without making a single direct statement, Eliot thus constructs all his ideas in the form of concrete images which do their work by their impact on the reader's *senses*, making him *feel* the force of the abstract ideas behind the passage.

In *The Waste Land* the poet illustrates especially the break with tradition—in religion, in contacts with the soil, in literary culture—which is starving and draining the world of its essential spiritual nourishment. Man is isolated from everything which gave him dignity and stability. He is simply a unit in a crowd, no longer a living part of a living organic social system. He is 'fear in a handful of dust'; he is

> Your shadow at morning striding behind you
> Or your shadow at evening rising to meet you.

The world of the 'Unreal City,' of 'crowds of people walking around in a ring,' of dirty and depressing urban aridity, breaks into every memory of past faiths, of the natural rhythm of the seasons and the abundance of nature. Any memory of the past is intercepted and transformed into a realization of the shoddiness and the triviality of the present, just as an echo of the love poetry of a former age will be intercepted and transformed in the same way:

> But at my back from time to time I hear
> The sound of horns and motors, which shall bring
> Sweeney to Mrs. Porter in the spring.

* For a complete interpretation of this difficult but, as Baedeker would say, 'rewarding' poem, the reader is referred to *A Dialogue of Modern Poetry* by Ruth Bailey (Oxford University Press).

Everywhere he feels the dreariness, ugliness, noise and dirt, fogs and smells, of modern urban conditions; the vulgarities and falsities and sterility and sheer boredom of modern love; the impotence and cheap quackery of modern values. He is haunted with longings and memories of the old richness of faith and art and humanity; of the glories of romance and the ample worlds of the great saints and teachers and poets and dramatists; of the beauty and refreshment of the world of nature. But those worlds are only shards of what was once a living whole, 'a heap of broken images,' 'withered stumps of time': the towers from which they pealed messages of aspiration and hope are now upside down,

Tolling reminiscent bells, that kept the hours
And voices singing out of empty cisterns and exhausted
    wells.

In many of the earlier poems the same torturing multi-plicity of vision is presented: contrasts between rotting animal bodies and living thought; between the emotional starvation of formal religion and the ecstasy of medieval faith; between the potentialities of a Shakespeare and the capacity of a Mr. Prufrock measuring out life with coffee spoons. And the human beings who people these poems are, too, emblems of the modern world, and of the feeble, bestial, unfruitful relationships of men and women in it: 'Apeneck' Sweeney and his female associates, Doris and Mrs. Porter; the sensitive, futile Mr. Prufrock; the ego-tistical 'Lady' and her spurious culture; Bleistein and the Princess Volupine, with her 'meagre, blue-nailed phthisic hand'; Grishkin and her friendly bust, with its 'promise of pneumatic bliss'; the typist and 'the young man carbuncular'; Madame Sosostris with her 'wicked pack of cards,' the symbol of the empty superstition which has replaced a living faith. Every portrait is startlingly actual in itself, and by his subtle use of allusion and quotation, against these actualities Eliot invokes the shadows and memories of what men and women have been—of Agamemnon and Hamlet, Mark Antony and Othello, Donne and Dante; of Cleopatra, Desdemona and Juliet, of Nausicaa and Beatrice.

§

> We think of the key, each in his prison
> Thinking of the key.

'The question *how to live* . . . is the question which most interests everyone, and with which, in some way or other, he is perpetually occupied.' *

These quotations (which might serve as an illustration in brief of the difference between the use of an image to convey a thought and the use of an intellectual concept) present a truth which is fundamental to human nature. Eliot in his early poems provides no key, but the poetry is a creation, brilliant and profound, of the prison. And it is a prison doubly locked. For not only can the poet find no escape in establishing any sympathetic contact between himself and his environment, but he can find no escape from the disorder of his own spirit. *The Waste Land* ends:

> Datta. Dayadhvam. Damyata.
> Shantih shantih shantih

* Matthew Arnold.

Give. Sympathize. Control. 'The Peace which passeth understanding.' But this is the cry of a soul that cannot use the words as a foundation of faith, but only as some of the fragments he has shored against his ruins. The mood, however, is not entirely negative. There are hints that the poet's spiritual death may be a prelude to a rebirth. The surrender in the *Death by Water* section recalls the rite in which an image of the fertility god was cast into the seas and later recovered as a symbol of the death and rebirth of summer. The constant references to *The Tempest*, too, are significant. For that play deals with supposed drowning and apparent death, which results in a personal and national regeneration.

Eliot gives no explicit criticism of the modern world. The method, as well as the theme, of *The Waste Land* is that of *Gerontion*. But it is even more complex and baffling, for in addition to the picture of a dying civilization, the poem includes the personal response of the poet to this condition. Not only the *thing*, but himself in relation to the thing is his subject matter. The composition of the poem is a landscape of the soul. He quotes a passage from F. H. Bradley's *Appearance and Reality*, in the notes to *The Waste Land*, which focuses the viewpoint:

My external sensations are no less private to myself than are my thoughts and feelings. In either case my experience falls within my own circle, a circle closed on the outside; and with all its elements alike, every sphere is opaque to the others which surround it. . . . In brief, regarded as an existence which appears in a soul, the whole world for each is peculiar and private to that soul.

The unity of the poem is the unity of this circle; and this conditions the form, which is never that of the *de-*

velopment of a theme, but that of *variations* on a theme.
When this is grasped, the apparent disorder of the movement is seen to be part of a different kind of order, not
the order of *progression*, but the order of *synthesis*. The
amount of material synthesized is bewildering in its variety: symbols of impotence, sterility, inhibition, and
others of fertility and freedom; memories and associations of religions, literatures, cults; realistic figures, moments of intense personal emotion, scenes of beauty, scenes
of horror, scenes of nightmare hallucination, of gentle
reverie, of dramatic realism. All this is enclosed in a mind
which responds to its experience in gusts of despair, defeat, ironic contempt, pity, nostalgic regret and longing,
terror, exhaustion, and tortured sensibility.

It is the whole conscious and subconscious mind of
one sensitive and intelligent human creature, arranged by
an original artist into an integer composed of bewildering
fractions. But the picture of the mind of this one tormented artist is also the revelation of the plight of an
epoch.

§

The work of the poet whose name is most commonly
coupled with that of Eliot, Ezra Pound, provides a further
illustration and commentary on 'the spirit of the age.' The
two poets write out of the same atmosphere and of it, but
their spirit as well as approach are completely different.
While Eliot's method is visionary, Pound's is critical;
while Eliot is evocative, Pound is provocative. Eliot includes himself in his vision of the world's collapse, he is
discouraged and humble; Pound stands outside what he

is criticizing, he is contentious and combative. 'Go,' he says to his books, 'Go out and defy opinion,'

> Greet the grave and the stodgy
> Salute them with your thumbs at your noses.

His *Cantos*, he says, are an *histoire morale contemporaine*. We might say the same of *The Waste Land*, but no two poems could be more unlike in essentials. Both use a jumble of material. The *Cantos* are a mosaic of translation, historical anecdote, quotation, economic discussion, and lyrical description, dealing mainly with the Greek and Latin classics, medieval France, Renaissance Italy and modern England and America. Instead of Eliot's method of a structure of suggestive images, Pound uses far more often a structure of factual instances and statistics, which interpret and illumine his thesis. His characters, too, instead of being carefully selected and concentrated symbols, are a mixed company of classical gods, heroes and poets, Chinese sages, Italian princes, pontiffs and art patrons, armament makers, gangsters, bankers and politicians. He does not create or suggest the shoddiness of political and cultural standards by innuendo and implication, as Eliot does; his criticism is direct and pugnacious:

> There died a myriad,
> And of the best, among them,
> For an old bitch gone in the teeth,
> For a botched civilization.

Like Eliot, he emphasizes the debased values of the modern world obliquely by placing them in juxtaposition to those of the past—to those of Confucius, Homer, Ovid, the troubadours, Virgil and Dante; but unlike Eliot, he points no less grimly to the sameness of violence, trickery, corruption and egotism in all ages. Whereas Eliot sees the origin of the modern collapse in the decay of tradition, Pound sees it in the ascendancy of financial jobbery. All too often, he blunts his satire by mere wasteful and strident denunciation, but his method of ironic juxtaposition, with its sharp malicious edge to it, is sometimes very effective. It can be seen very well in Canto XVIII. Here, with dry astringent humor he places parallel instances of human cupidity and cunning taken from the thirteenth and the twentieth centuries, leaving them to speak for themselves. His object of attack is war-profiteering, and the poem opens with an extract from a letter of Marco Polo describing the Emperor Kublai's invention of paper money, and how by this device he enriched himself at the expense of both foreign traders and his own nobles. The transition from this to the prosperity of munition makers is accomplished by two inconsequential remarks illustrating the triviality of the concept of national honor and the delusion that conquest necessarily brings prosperity:

> There was a boy in Constantinople
> And some Britisher kicked his arse.
> 'I hate these french,' said Napoleon, aged 12.
> To young Bourrienne, 'I will do them all the harm that
> I can.'

The traffic in munitions is then introduced directly and explosively, with a mixture of leering horse-laughter and mock gravity.

> 'Peace! Pieyce!!' said Mr. Giddings,
> 'Uni-ver-sal? Not while yew got tew billions ov money,'

Said Mr. Giddings, 'invested in the man-u-facture
'Of war machinery. Haow I sold it to Russia—
'Well we tuk 'em a new torpedo-boat,
'And it was all electric, run it all from a
'Little bit uv a keyboard, about like the size ov
'A typewriter, and the prince come aboard,
'An' we sez wud yew like to run her?
'And he run damn slam on the breakwater,
'And bust off all her front end,
'And he was my gawd scared out of his panties.
'Who wuz agoin' tew pay for the damage?
'And it was my first trip out fer the company,
'And I sez, yer highness, it is nothing,
'We will give yew a new one. And, my Christ!
'The company backed me, and did we get a few orders?'

To put this story, in the form of a salesman's boastful
garrulity, side by side with Marco Polo's reports of human
cupidity of seven hundred years earlier is typical of
Pound's sharp sense of extravagant correspondences.

While Pound has many happy effects of external dramatic contrast of this sort, he has, however, none of Eliot's
power of evoking a sense of drama below the level of the
external action. We need only compare Pound's *Portrait
d'une Femme* with *Portrait of a Lady*, or Poem XII in the
Hugh Selwyn Mauberley sequence with *The Love Song of
J. Alfred Prufrock*, to see the difference between the critical and the creative treatment of similar themes. And Pound
entirely lacks that sense of inner dramatic tension which
integrates even the most obscure passages of *The Waste
Land*. There we feel the drama of a human soul in conflict
with itself and its environment. The substance of the
poem is an inner struggle, while that of the *Cantos* is
external observation. Both poets are bitterly antagonistic
to modern civilization. Eliot, however, in his early poems

is haunted by his failure to find a foothold in it, while Pound is sure of himself, sure of his own superior position. When Pound describes hell in Cantos XIV and XV, he creates none of the spiritual horror we feel in the atmosphere of *Gerontion*, for instance, that sense of mingled revulsion and pity before the vision of human wickedness and weakness. Pound, exhilarated by antipathies, pours out a stream of cloacal invective against individuals whom he dislikes. It is in no sense a vision of man's soul, it is a cesspool of grotesquely revengeful wish-fulfillment. As Eliot himself said of it:

I find one considerable objection to a Hell of this sort: that a Hell altogether without dignity implies a Heaven without dignity also. . . . Mr. Pound's Hell, for all its horrors, is a perfectly comfortable one for the modern mind to contemplate, and disturbing to no one's complacency: it is a Hell for the *other* people, the people we read about in the newspapers, not for oneself and one's friends.

And as Pound's sense of evil is of the surface, so is his vision of human good. While he is full of hatred of modern society, he is himself typical of its weakness. He is rootless. He can re-create the spirit of a past civilization, in the form of translation and adaptation, with the most delicate deftness of touch, as he does in *Cathay* or in *Homage to Sextus Propertius*, but he cannot accept any culture of the past as a way of life in the present. And having no roots in any other culture, either national or religious, he has manufactured for himself a synthetic culture, based on the product of his own vast reading. But a man may possess a great many tags of culture without in the end belonging to any fundamental culture, just as he may have baggage covered with a great many foreign hotel labels without in the end being fundamentally cosmopolitan. Learning makes us aware of other cultures, but it cannot create a culture, which is a matter of growth and tradition and heritage. Pound's culture is that of the exiled dilettante. It is a private eclectic culture which gleans fragments of wisdom, history, art and economic theory from all ages, irrespective of the soil in which they grew or of the faiths which made them live. As Eliot said of him: 'he is attracted to the Middle Ages apparently by everything except that which gives them their significance.' And inevitably the possession of this kind of culture generates that sense of difference from, and superiority to, ordinary men, and the complacency about that difference and superiority, which we have already noted as a symptom of the loss of community feeling in the poet. It is the culture of a man of taste and leisure living in an intellectual isolation. 'I mate with my free kind upon the crags.'

There is a passage in Canto XI which describes the scope and content of a Renaissance conversation:

'Both of ancient times and our own; books, arms,
And of men of unusual genius,
Both of ancient times and our own, in short the usual
    subjects
Of conversation between intelligent men.'

This is an excellent summing up of Pound's poetry; but even with a winnowed audience of intelligent men his 'culture' is a stumbling block to communication, and the pot-pourri of languages in which the verse is served up irritates the mental membranes instead of stimulating them, and weakens instead of reinforcing the experience and themes which it presents. His sterling becomes de-valuated. Again and again passages of delicately executed rhythm and imagery are all but stifled between chunks of Italian, Latin and Greek and an overlay of mythologi-cal allusion. When he is automatically prevented from bursting out into the original tongue, as in the poems in *Cathay*, or in Canto XIII, the verse gains enormously in simplicity and directness.

> And Kung said, and wrote on the bo leaves:
>   If a man have not order within him
> He can not spread order about him;
> And if a man have not order within him
> His family will not act with due order;
>   And if the prince have not order within him
> He can not put order in his dominions.
> And Kung gave the words 'order'
> And 'brotherly deference'
> And said nothing of the 'life after death.'
> And he said
>   'Anyone can run to excesses,
> It is easy to shoot past the mark,
> It is hard to stand firm in the middle.'

This passage illustrates, too, Pound's greatest achieve-ment: his mastery of a verse which uses the speech idiom as its basis, and can present a wide range of emotional and intellectual material in a medium which never loses the tone of easy, cultivated conversation. Pound is a master of many meters, but it is this type of verse which he dis-covered anew and perfected for his own age, and it is his great gift to the poetry of today. Just as Spenser was 'the poet's poet' of the romantics, so Pound is the poet's poet of an age of poet-craftsmen. Compared with Eliot he has very little 'substance' of his own. All his best work is in adaptation, when the substance is already given, and he can apply his critical discipline to a reworking of it in his own felicity of diction, to a sharpening of edge and a polishing of surface. In these technical matters there is scarcely a serious verse-writer of the last twenty years who does not owe him a direct debt, and he and Eliot between them revolutionized the poetic use of the English language.

Both poets diagnosed the social situation of their own day and themselves illustrate it. Both are expatriates, drawing no nourishment from a national culture. One has now found harmony in a traditional religious culture; the other remains a patchwork. He has not developed; he remains a man with a brilliant future behind him. But both played their part in revealing the age to itself: both gave their readers new eyes. If Eliot awakened them to a new orientation by his fresh plotting of the psychological landscape, Pound provoked their thinking by the sharp worm-prodding beak of his satiric intelligence. And both gave readers not only new eyes but new ears. If in their substance they illustrate the death of the old ways of living and the break with the social cultures of the past, in their practice they illustrate the liveliness of the poetic tradition and its capacity for growth and continuity. While Eliot revealed a fresh medium of communication in his evocative use of image, Pound revealed a no less fresh one by the disciplined skill with which he used the language of speech as the language of verse. Together they perfected the ways of expression to which the whole of contemporary poetry owes its particular character, and dug the technical channels into which it was to flow.

CHAPTER 3

The Nineteen Twenties

> . . . the age into which I was born, in spite of its
> lavishness of entertainment, has been intellectually
> and morally in perfect confusion.
>
> ROBERT GRAVES. (b. 1895)

> We had been born with illusions, unlike the present
> generation, but having lost them at a very early age,
> we felt the need of replacing them with others;
> and we had come to erect the sordid into a kind of
> religion.
>
> MALCOLM COWLEY. (b. 1898)

> Poor Richard Lovat wearied himself to death
> struggling with the problem of himself and calling
> it Australia.
>
> D. H. LAWRENCE. *Kangaroo.* (1923)

YEATS, writing of the memory of all that Lady Gregory and Coole Park represented for him, said:

> We were the last romantics—chose for theme
> Traditional sanctity and loveliness;
> Whatever's written in what poets name
> The book of the people; whatever most can bless
> The mind of man or elevate a rhyme;
> But all is changed, that high horse riderless . . .

But though 'romance' as poetic material had been dying long before Yeats wrote this, it was not dead even in the nineteen twenties. There is an exotic romanticism in Roy Campbell's *The Zebras:*

> From the dark woods that breathe of fallen showers,
> Harnessed with level rays in golden reins,

The zebras draw the dawn across the plains
Wading knee-deep among the scarlet flowers.
The sunlight, zithering their flanks with fire,
Flashes between the shadows as they pass
Barred with electric tremors through the grass
Like wind along the gold strings of a lyre.

Into the flushed air snorting rosy plumes
That smoulder round their feet in drifting fumes,
With dove-like voices call the distant fillies,
While round the herds the stallion wheels his flight,
Engine of beauty volted with delight,
To roll his mare among the trampled lilies.

This is full of positive vitality, and so is his long poem
The Flaming Terrapin, with its resonant fresco rhetoric.
The same drive and exuberance of speech colors with a
darker tinge the crude melodramas of Robinson Jeffers.
Hart Crane's reckless undisciplined swirl of words is essentially romantic; so is the poetry of Cummings, though
sometimes he masks it under a surface satire and a stencil-
ing of unfamiliar formal pattern. But 'traditional sanctity
and loveliness' is not the phrase we should choose to
describe what we have been accustomed to call 'post-war'
poetry. The epithet embodied disillusion. But perhaps
'post-Eliot' would point the direction better, for it is in
the minor poets of the nineteen twenties that we find
elaborated the physical, emotional and moral picture of
which Eliot had first made the age conscious. 'You track
him everywhere in their snow,' as Dryden said of Ben
Jonson and his disciples.

§

'Hurrah for positive science!' Walt Whitman had sung;
but the next generation was not to echo him. It is true

that Hart Crane could chant the glories of the new forces
let loose within the universe:

> The nasal whine of power whips a new universe . . .
> Where spouting pillars spoor the evening sky,
> Under the looming stacks of the gigantic power house
> Stars prick the eyes with sharp ammoniac proverbs,
> New verities, new inklings in the velvet hummed
> Of dynamos, where hearing's leash is strummed . . .
> Power's script,—wound, bobbin-bound, refined—
> Is stropped to the slap of belts on booming spools. . .

But it was rather the horror of the industrialized urban
civilization resulting from the new powers which affected
the minds of the new poets: a hatred of the popular idea
that progress could be equated with plumbing, and might
be summed up as an infinite capacity for making drains;
a conviction that the old order was lost.

> The sun no longer shares our works
> And the earth is alive with creeping men
> Mechanical beetles never quite warm.*

D. H. Lawrence called them 'insipid, unsalted, rabbitty,
endlessly-hopping creatures.'

　The poems of the intelligentsia are all painfully conscious of the social dilemma and of their own sense of
insecurity. They see themselves isolated in a world ravaged
and exhausted by war, made hideous by commercialism
and vulgarized by wealth.

> Inexpressible itching to be photographed
> with Lord Rothermere playing
> with Lord Rothermere billiards
> very well by moonlight with
> Lord Rothermere.†

* Wallace Stevens.
† E. E. Cummings.

Variations on the theme of the loss of past faiths provide a haunting and ubiquitous refrain, echoed by Raymond Larsson in *The Inward-Turning Eye.*

                    Heavy the lid
          of sky
                  the heavy lidded eye
          of sky turns inward—
                                      inward
          the inner eye
                          inward on the vast
          grey vapours
          of a decomposing past

This is matched by the theme of the decay and deadness of the present. The atmosphere of Allen Tate's conversation piece *The Oath* is eloquent of death. A bullet-mold, a powder-horn and a soldier's portrait—relics of a vital past—comment on the present:

          There's naught to kill but the animated dead.

                    .   .   .   .

          Then Lytle asked: Who are the dead?
          Who are the living and the dead?
          And nothing more was said. . . .

The tone of the age is as pessimistic as Hardy's, but there is none of Hardy's energetic skepticism and solid unmitigated acceptance of the cruelty of the universe. Nor is it the sense of anger and irony such as we feel behind the war poetry of Wilfred Owen or Robert Graves. It is the futility not of dying but of living which obsesses these young poets. Roy Campbell sums up the literary atmosphere bluntly:

          Love-shattered bards, cuckolds whose heads are sore,
          And disillusioned novelists galore,
          Who blame it all upon the poor old War.

Certainly a kind of low-spiritual blood-pressure afflicts a great number of poets. Frustrate and hopeless, badgered by personal emotional conflicts, floundering in maladjustments, they examine their lives under the emotional microscope of the individual identity; feeling, like Conrad Aiken, just 'an absurd cocoon of consciousness hung in the void'; or asking, like Archibald MacLeish, 'How shall we learn what it is our hearts believe in?' No contacts of the flesh can allay the fever of the bone, no ecstasy liberates the shackled spirit: 'all thoughts to rive the heart are there and all are vain.'

§

However, certain of the poets of the nineteen twenties were of sufficient stature to react in strongly individual manners to the general influences of the time. Indeed, the prevailing spirit of doubt and questioning encouraged a self-conscious individualism. In ages of stability, poets can take themselves for granted—and the relationship between themselves and society for granted—just as we take health for granted when our bodies are functioning harmoniously. At such times we express our personalities unself-consciously, live freely and positively in the present, and look forward hopefully to the future. It is in periods of sickness that we feel nostalgia for happier days, and become introspective, critical and acutely aware of personal idiosyncrasies.

We may say that the poetry of this age is markedly idiosyncratic, and that in the main the poets are actively at variance with the society of which they form a part. But there are certain poets, very different in themselves, writing at this period, whose inspiration appears to be unaffected by any of the attitudes or influences which impede their fellow workers. Of these, one, Robert Frost, is probably the most widely read poet of the time. Frost's poetry has for most readers the initial advantage of being grounded in a familiar environment. There is nothing in its content or its expression which demands any forcible readjustment of vision. Frost's achievement is that he rarely leaves that accepted vision exactly as it was before.

He has obvious affinities with Wordsworth, and to a less degree with Hardy, while his isolation from the fashions of his own day is seen at once in the character of his language. This can at times be dull and pedestrian, and frequently he deliberately flattens its tone, so that its heartbeat is almost as faint as that of the verse of Wordsworth's *Michael;* but few writers have produced naturalistic conversation in verse with more successful realism, or naturalistic description with sharper detail. He is entirely untouched by the current influences of the Symbolists and the Metaphysicals. The way of experiencing life which demands those techniques is not his way. But in view of the attacks on modern obscurity it is interesting to note that Frost has written lines as tortured and elliptical in their simplicity as those of any complex modern. Take these from *Maple:*

> It was as personal as he could be
> About the way he saw it was with you
> To say your mother, had she lived, would be
> As far again as from being born to bearing.

But in general Frost's method of presenting his response to living is the traditional method of the older poets. He

embodies it mainly in fable, parable and soliloquy, sometimes adding an interpretative comment, sometimes allow-
ing the facts to speak for themselves. His attitude to his
New England environment is that of a man who participates to the full in its life. He is a practical farmer, never
forgetting that life has a material basis which cannot be
ignored. His comment on finding the deserted woodpile is
characteristic.

> I thought that only
> Someone who lived in turning to fresh tasks
> Could so forget his handiwork on which
> He spent himself, the labour of his axe,
> And leave it there far from a useful fireplace
> To warm the frozen swamp as best it could
> With the slow smokeless burning of decay.

'The fact is the sweetest dream that labor knows,' he
says in *Mowing*, and he makes his poetry out of the fact,
exactly as he sees it.

> The view was all in lines
> Straight up and down of tall slim trees
> Too much alike to mark or name a place by
> So as to say for certain I was here
> Or somewhere else; *

He has the keenest eye for every detail of the country-
side, seeing the fallen leaves fitting the earth like a glove,
or noting the lumps of gum,

> Like uncut jewels, dull and rough.
> It comes to market golden brown;
> But turns to pink between the teeth.

or marking the birches after an icestorm:

* *The Woodpile.*

> They click upon themselves
> As the breeze rises, and turn many-colored
> As the stir cracks and crazes their enamel.

And his vision of human nature is similar. He makes no sentimental evasions, he is rooted in realities, he reports the fact. In the story called *Out, Out—*, for example, of the boy whose hand was cut off by the buzz-saw, and who dies under the ether, he concludes:

> that ended it.
> No more to build on there. And they, since they
> Were not the one dead, turned to their affairs.

The interest of the facts to the readers of Frost is that the facts are told to us by a man who is not only completely honest, but possesses an original mind and a rare spiritual sincerity. Frost is simple, but he is not at all innocent. He has a sturdy rationalism.

> Before I built a wall I'd ask to know
> What I was walling in or walling out
> And to whom I was like to give offence.

His attitude of ironic detachment never deserts him, so that though he is sometimes dull, he is never mawkish, and though he is deeply moral, he is never didactic. He writes out of an assured spiritual harmony which has nothing superficial or facile about it, but which is the result of a courageous acceptance of circumstances. *The Oven Bird* is a revealing poem:

> The bird would cease and be as other birds
> But that he knows in singing not to sing.
> The question that he frames in all but words
> Is what to make of a diminished thing.

Frost is not 'as other birds' in a narrow environment. He transforms that environment in his best poetry not by an intensity or a transcendancy of vision, but rather by a subdued strength of understatement: 'he knows in singing not to sing.' And of his 'diminished thing' he has made a world lighted by such quiet geniality, simple robust faith in earth, delicate sensibility, human and humorous sympathy and shrewdness, whimsical grimness and realistic wisdom, that it is no wonder he is beloved of the reading public.

§

Two other poets of distinction who are unself-conscious about the modern social environment are both women—Laura Riding and Marianne Moore. Like Frost, they also criticize life, but not contemporary life. Laura Riding is a rigidly disciplined metaphysician in verse, and Marianne Moore a subtle, graceful observer.

In her essay *Poetry and the Literary Universe*, published in 1928, Laura Riding denounced 'the gospel of contemporaneity,' and professed her faith in detachment from contemporary social sentiment and the canons of *contemporary* criticism. While her fellow poets of this period were deliberately or indeliberately reflecting in their work the spirit of the age, she was decrying the subjection of the creative spirit to a time-sense criticism which required poetry 'to proceed not from an individual sense of life but from a social sense of literature.' She concludes that 'the poetic intelligence must fight alone against the aggressions of the concrete intelligence and at times of intense synthesizing like the present, is even forced to disappear from itself or to cover its tracks with the dry leaves of philosophical sentiment.'

However arbitrary this prescription may seem in a long-range view of poetry, it is an illuminating commentary on the direction Miss Riding's individualism has taken. 'Harsh, bare and matter-of-fact,' her poetry is sometimes pared down to the very vanishing point of articulate expression. It is intensely subjective, and almost every verse she has written crackles with 'philosophical sentiment.' She manipulates a most austere and economic technique, rigidly concentric (as opposed to the relaxed eccentric movement of Marianne Moore's poetry) and extremely limited in its range of rhythms and image. But it is on her substantial accomplishment that she must be judged. She has mastered a technique of 'tender exiguity' in modern metaphysical poetry which sufficiently justifies her claims for the 'individual sense of life' in poetic expression:

> Then I heard little leaves in my ears rustling
> And a little wind like a leaf blowing
> My mind into a corner of my mind,
> Where wind over empty ground went blowing
> And a large dwarf picked and picked up nothing.

Despite its gentle charm and sly careful humor, Marianne Moore's poetry does not establish the direct contact between itself and general humanity which is the secret of Frost's popularity. Her audience will always be small. She speaks to a few—as cat to cat, we might say, remembering her tender observation of those delightfully astringent creatures, saying, women have charm, and how annoying they can be.

or

> The passion for setting people right is in itself an afflic-
> tive disease.
> Distaste which takes no credit to itself is best.

But in spite of her astringency, it would be difficult to find anyone less self-assertive than Marianne Moore:

> What is
> there in being able
> to say that one has dominated the stream in an attitude
> of self-defence;
> in proving that one has had the experience
> of carrying a stick?

'Snobbishness is stupidity,' she says, and again,

> Could
> not all personal upheaval in
> the name of freedom, be tabooed?

She prefers a cool detached impersonality of expression. Her sympathy is with Mount Tacoma,

> damned for its sacrosanct remoteness—
> like Henry James 'damned by the public for decorum';
> not decorum, but restraint;
> it is the love of doing hard things
> that rebuffed and wore them out—a public out of
> sympathy
> with neatness.
> Neatness of finish! Neatness of finish!
> Relentless accuracy is the nature of this octopus
> with its capacity for fact.

Here Marianne Moore, in her characteristic manner, brings together a group of facts, concepts and images very fruitful for a consideration of her own work; for almost everything which is most significant about herself is included in it. Remoteness is sacred to her too, and is the cause of her apparent coldness; but it does not imply either obscurity or 'superiority.' It is part of an instinctive aristocratic quietism. Her vision is never turned inwards in tortured self-analysis, but neither is it that of a self-conscious sophistication and 'the perfunctory heart':

> sophistication is as it al-
> ways has been—at the antipodes from the init-
> ial great truths.

And she thoroughly dislikes the cult of complexity for its own sake:

> complexity is not a crime, but carry
> it to the point of murki-
> ness and nothing is plain.

At the root of her work is a healthy dislike of humbug, of insensitiveness, of pedantic literalism, and of all kinds of human aggressiveness. *When I Buy Pictures* is illuminating, with its conclusion:

> Too stern an intellectual emphasis upon this quality
> or that
> detracts from one's enjoyment.
> It must not wish to disarm anything; nor may the ap-
> proved triumph easily be honoured—
> that which is great because something else is small.
> It comes to this: of whatever sort it is,
> it must be 'lit with piercing glances into the life of
> things';
> it must acknowledge the spiritual forces which have
> made it.

Impersonality and restraint, 'unconscious fastidiousness,' are the spiritual forces which are most apparent in her own poetry. We must be able to experience 'the intensity of the mood' behind it, undismayed by its lack of personal warmth and its inexorable externality. Yet her 'piercing glances into the life of things' are apparent everywhere. It is not the comprehensive vision of the greatest poetry, it is criticism of significant features in the scene: of aesthetics, marriage, statecraft, poetry, human types, New York and America. It is criticism without a hint of self-assertion, but full of the self-assurance of civilized and stable judgment. The piercing glance flashes into vivid epigrams or exquisitely sensitive descriptions of flowers, animals and natural objects, and widens outward into a rich pattern of association.

She is difficult because she will not buy triumph at 'horrifying sacrifice of stringency'; she refuses to descend to the level of those to whom 'the illustration is nothing without the application'; and she demands of her readers that their minds shall follow hers in leaping by fifths and sevenths from point to point like the jerboa in her poem. She has affinities of spirit with Henry James—the same thoroughness and elegant restraint, the same astute detection of minute differences, the same gradual foliate disclosure and sharp clarity of definition. But all these qualities are condensed into the 'contractility' of verse. Her subtlety of ear and delicacy of rhythmic perception, the variations in her use of full, light, vowel, end, and internal rhymes, and her ingenious designs of syllabic division, are all functional parts of the setting in which she arranges her brilliant 'jewelry of sense.'

§

In spite of the dissimilarity between the poetry of these three poets—Frost, Laura Riding and Marianne Moore—they have some characteristics in common. All are restrained, ironic and witty, and all write from a position of intellectual stability in a world of shifting values. But in their ways of experiencing and their ways of writing they face in entirely different directions.

Their individualism is the unself-conscious expression of clearly defined and harmonious personalities; but the idiosyncrasies of most of the minor poets of this period have that touch of conscious emphasis which arises from a sense of maladjustment to an environment, and divorce from communal interests. E. E. Cummings, Wallace Stevens and John Crowe Ransom react towards this situation in terms of irony. Hart Crane had perhaps a more natural and vigorous poetic genius than any of these. But he was incapable of a sustained irony, which might have provided an inclusive attitude harmonizing his vision of actuality, his romantic transcendentalism and his personal neuroses. His natural power of poetic expression was prodigious, but its effectiveness was defeated by his uncertainty of technical control. This accounts for his essential 'patchiness,' his exasperating combination of the meritorious and the meretricious. In poems such as *Voyages, Repose of Rivers, For the Marriage of Faustus and Helen*, in spite of their obscurities, the language and rhythm produce an immediacy of emotional effect. His extraordinary stirring and kindling power with words is most manifest in scattered lines which shoot suddenly like a rocket from dark surroundings:

> In alternating bells have you not heard
> All hours clapped dense into a single stride?

or

> Down Wall, from girder into street noon leaks,
> A rip-tooth of the sky's acetylene.

But a careful rereading of Crane leaves the impression that in the main he viewed experience not through the eye or the mind, but through a vocabulary. His genius was a mixed, insecure, half-realized genius for evocative statement through the associative colors, shapes and reverberations of words. New accessions in words held an irresistible fascination for him. He fancied himself as welcoming the unused and the unexplored in experience, 'New soothings, new amazements,' 'New thresholds, new anatomies,' 'New verities, new inklings'; but it was really the unused and unexplored in words which attracted him. The new thresholds opened always onto some vague transcendental experience which had no basis in clear thinking or controlled feeling. He employed words merely as an excitant, blurring all coherent vision in confused declamatory resonance. The conclusion of *The Bridge* is an example:

> So to thine Everpresence, beyond time,
> Like spears ensanguined of one tolling star
> That bleeds infinity—the orphic strings,
> Sidereal phalanxes, leap and converge;

Crane's essential weakness, indeed, is revealed in his pathetic attempt to attain epic stature in *The Bridge*.

R. P. Blackmur, in his essay on Crane, speaking of the failure of the long poem in the present age, writes:

It is a striking and disheartening fact that the three most ambitious poems of our time should all have failed in similar ways: in composition, in independent objective existence, and in intelligibility of language.

He points out that each of these three poems—*The Waste Land*, Pound's *Cantos* and *The Bridge*—requires the reader to supply from outside the poem the important, controlling part of the 'meaning'; and he compares this demand with the method of the long poem in all previous ages, when the great poet was always 'rational, integrating, a master of ultimate verbal clarity.' Crane's deficiency in ultimate verbal clarity was the natural result of his deficiency in clarity of conception.

Dr. Johnson once wrote:

There are two things that I am confident I can do very well. One is an introduction to any literary work, stating what it is to contain, and how it should be executed in the most perfect manner. The other is a conclusion shewing from various causes why the execution has not been equal to what the author promised to himself and to the publick.

Crane was an adept at the first achievement, and it has remained for his critics sadly to perform the second office for him. In a letter to Otto Kahn, he outlined the scope of his work, pointing out how each section had its own problem of form and was related to the major design of the whole poem. He compared its structure in one place to the tableaux of the Sistine Chapel, and in another to the *Aeneid*, and adds: 'In more than one sense I feel justified in comparing the historical and cultural scope of *The Bridge* to that great work.' Crane did himself a disservice by such comparisons, for they only emphasize the chaos of his own effort.

Crane's temperament, that of the romantic egotist, was the worst possible equipment for a poet of the nineteen twenties. The majority of his fellow poets resorted to irony as an escape from the unsympathetic atmosphere in which they found themselves during this period. Some interesting examples of this attitude may be seen in the poetry of Wallace Stevens and John Crowe Ransom.

§

The irony of Stevens is less pervasive than that of Ransom, and the flavor of the two poets is quite different. Neither concerns himself directly with the modern social scene, nor is often immediately personal. Both are objective, holding their material at a distance and observing it critically from oblique angles. But Stevens shifts his focus more frequently, and has developed a wider variety of approach.

His early work proved his fresh lyric gift, and a particular competence in the light 'little language' of lyrical rhythms. Poetry, he says, 'is a finikin thing of air'

> That lives uncertainly and not for long
> Yet radiantly beyond much lustier blurs.

The light in which his early writing moves is reflected in this conceit. That is not to say that the poetry is poor in thought, but rather that its mechanics compose a tone and feeling of lightness and brightness and airiness and oddness which are peculiar to him and a personal world of his own.

> I was the world in which I walked and what I saw
> Or heard or felt came not but from myself,
> And there I found myself more truly and more strange.

Within the boundaries of this world he skips between serious reflection, nostalgic sentiment and whimsical, moonlit satire. And as an added oddness a suggestion of improvisation flashes through the 'abundant zone' which serves as décor; a volatile nonchalance which expresses itself in loose singing rhythms, accidental rhymes, with a humming and strumming accompaniment of fanciful spelled-out sounds. *The Ordinary Women* is a good example.

Stevens' most important work thus far has been in reflective satire. It is interesting to compare his attitude in *The Comedian as the Letter C.* with Pound's *Hugh Selwyn Mauberley*. Stevens directs his irony at the individual artist and his failures, whereas Pound directs his at the age which fails to appreciate the artist:

> The 'age demanded' chiefly a mould in plaster,
> Made with no loss of time,
> A prose kinema, not, not assuredly, alabaster
> Or the 'sculpture' of rhyme.

Stevens' Crispin is concerned with the 'mythology of self.' He shifts his position from that of 'Man is the intelligence of his soil,' the idea that man is superior to his environment, to the opposite position that only in accepting his environment and learning from it can man fulfill himself:

his soil is man's intelligence.
That's better.

The conclusion reached in the poem is simply that the
world, the turnip, however regarded, remains 'the same
insoluble lump'; but the problem of the relation of the
man of imagination to the actuality of his surroundings
remains Stevens' main preoccupation. It is treated again
at length in *Owl's Clover*, where his final perception is of
the imagination as the artist's great instrument of *order* in
the imperfect universe. Earlier he had equated the imagination with moonlight, with the unreal, and had hoped
through that to find

> The liaison, the blessed liaison
> Between himself and his environment.

But he discovers the moonlight to be

> evasion, or, if not,
> A minor meeting, facile, delicate.

In *Sunday Morning* he had founded his faith on the *order*
of sun and earth and natural things; again, it is the *order*
of traditional spiritual faith which he values—the fact that
in it man hears

> the voices that were once
> The confusion of men's voices, intricate
> Made extricate by meanings, meanings made
> Into a music never touched to sound.

It is this same principle of order which he now feels to be
the heart of the reality of poetry.

> Oh! Blessed rage for order, pale Ramon,
> The maker's rage to order words of the sea,
> Words of the fragrant portals, dimly-starred,

And of ourselves and of our origins,
In ghostlier demarcations, keener sounds.

§

Individuality of voice creates the contrasts in poetry enjoyed by the critical mind. Satisfactory as each may be in itself, the poetry of Marianne Moore or Stevens or Crane is considerably enhanced by observing the variations in individuality between them. And to extract the fullest flavor from the poetry of John Crowe Ransom we should read it against the background of his contemporaries. Read in isolation, it will at first seem colorless, toneless and dry, for it lacks the brittle exotic brilliance of the early Stevens, the fine exploratory rhetoric of Marianne Moore and the exciting visual imagery of Crane. But considered against these more spectacular qualities its own contrasting excellences receive the setting and lighting they require. Seen thus, Ransom's hard-twisted ironies and melancholy elegance of wit contribute to modern poetry a peculiar vitality not found in his contemporaries.

Ransom is a romantic ironist in verse, and, like the lovers in his *Eclogue*,

one part love
And nine parts bitter thought.

He speaks in a low, reflective key, intently skeptical where he philosophizes or moralizes, quietly tender in the expression of private emotion. Where Crane would flood a verse with emotional imagery, Ransom uses a single image, molding it into several shapes. The final stanza of *Winter Remembered* is a good example of this technical economy:

> Dear love, these fingers that had known your touch,
> And tied our separate forces first together,
> Were ten poor idiot fingers not worth much,
> Ten frozen parsnips hanging in the weather.

The image of the fingers is treated in four different ways in these four lines. First there is the passive image of feeling, followed by an active image. The last two lines state the difference between the time when the lovers were together and the present separation. The one image is used throughout, but in forms which annul first the capacity for passive enjoyment and finally even the capacity for action, so that the poem ends on a note of despair more terrible because drained of thought and feeling by the metaphor.

Ransom's language can best be appreciated in contrast with the more ambiguous and full-bodied idiom common to contemporary poetry. He will write in a homely way:

> Autumn days in our section
> Are the most used-up thing on earth.

His simplicity and conciseness of phrase are maintained with dry, unbroken evenness except where he occasionally contrives a significant vocable impact or color by introducing an eloquent latinism, as in *Dead Boy*, for example:

> The little cousin is dead, by foul subtraction,
> A green bough from Virginia's aged tree,
> And neither the county kin love the transaction
> Nor some of the world of outer dark, like me.

Or again in *Vaunting Oak*,

> And the frail leaves of a season, which are susceptive
> Of the mad humours of wind, and turn and beat
> Ecstatic round the stem on which they are captive.

Just as 'subtraction' accurately describes death according to the special attitude of the poem in which it appears, 'susceptive' gives both sound and motion to the leaves in the second poem. Or he will introduce a fragment of dialect, as in *Here Lies a Lady*, where the plain personality of 'thole' confirms the simplicity and ease of its elegiac mood:

> Sweet ladies, long may ye bloom, and toughly I hope ye
>   may thole,
> But was she not lucky? In flowers and lace and mourn-
>   ing,
> In love and great honour we bade God rest her soul
> After six little spaces of chill, and six of burning.

Ransom's subject matter is as plain as the treatment he gives it. 'My scene is prose,' he says, 'this people and I are earthy.' His comments on the fragile private tragedies of *Miriam Tazewell, Miss Euphemia* and *John Whitesides' Daughter* are expressed with simple affectionate bluntness.

No pavilioned clipper ships appear on his horizon; no peculiarities, human or zoological, except the actors in an occasional allegory; no flashing tropical color nor tinkling lilt of harlequinade enter his theater. He reflects somberly on the inexorable duality of things, the gulf between the senses and the intellect, the body and the head; between the life of actuality and the life of contemplation; between scientific knowledge and imaginative vision; between the joys of childhood and adult self-torment. His irony is the most important single element in his poetry. It dictates the subdued key which is so much more susceptible of subtle economies of tone-change than a larger volume would be. It restricts his language to the simple, lucid forms which take on a special sheen and sharpness when an oddity is dropped in their midst or a film of archaism passed over them. It infuses humor into his philosophic reflections and tempers his occasional solemnities. It is not the surface irony which we meet in Cummings. Such irony sinks easily into sentimentality because the base beneath will not support its weight. Ransom's is an intellectual irony basic to the firmly constructed satire of such poets as *Armageddon, Grace, Captain Carpenter* and *Adventure This Side of Pluralism.* He is a finer craftsman than Crane, a more dexterous philosopher than Riding and the equal of Moore and Stevens in play of satiric wit. But he is narrower than the others in the spread of privilege he offers to the reader. Ransom leaves us with the feeling that he has said all that he intended to say in his poem. The others leave us with the feeling that they have implied more than they have explicitly stated. These are two different poetic effects: but a consummate expression can be achieved in either, according to the gifts of the artist.

CHAPTER 4

Poetry and Meaning

Our mental business is carried on in the same way
as the business of the state: a great deal of hard
work is done by agents who are not acknowledged.
GEORGE ELIOT

Poetry gives most pleasure when only generally
and not perfectly understood.
S. T. COLERIDGE

WHEN Mr. Boffin, discussing with Mr. Silas
Wegg the question of suitable remuneration
for his services as reader, suggested half-a-
crown a week, Mr. Wegg replied:

'As to the amount of strain upon the intellect now. Was
you thinking at all of poetry?'
'Would it come dearer?' Mr. Boffin asked.
'It would come dearer,' Mr. Wegg returned. 'For when
a person comes to grind off poetry night after night, it
is but right he should expect to be paid for its weakening
effect on his mind.'

Any average reader of English and American poetry
of the last twenty years has inevitably felt about poetry as
Mr. Wegg did. It appears, indeed, to have such a weakening effect on his mind that he cannot understand it at all.
To come fresh to the poetry of Eliot or Pound or Hart
Crane or Empson after a conventional training on the
poets of the last two hundred years is to experience a
sense of complete bafflement. What *are* these poets doing?
Is there really some basic difference between present and

past poetry which cuts off the lover of the past from participation in the present?

There has always been poetry which is difficult. It may
be so because, in order to understand it, the reader needs
actual knowledge of the image subject matter. Much of
Donne needs such elucidation. Or it may be that the reader's ignorance extends to the whole symbolism on which
a poem is based, as in Blake's *Prophetic Books*, Eliot's *Ash
Wednesday* or Yeats' *Byzantium*. Or the trouble may
arise from extreme compression of syntax or the elliptical
nature of the poet's use of language, as in the poetry of
Hopkins.

Then again, all that type of poetry called 'metaphysical' offers another type of difficulty. It is the cause of the
commonest kind of obscurity in modern verse, that of
concentrated and condensed metaphor. Although this always makes for difficulty, it often has an explosive force,
even before its logical implications are realized, which
makes it particularly powerful and brilliant. Examples
will be analyzed later in this book. Many of its modern
exponents, however, do seem to forget that poetic beauty
is a pied beauty, a dappled thing; one does not want it so
weighted down with density of meaning that it cannot
use its wings. Moreover modern metaphysical verse is
extremely enigmatic, much more so than its seventeenth
century ancestor. It is its nature to be complex, since its
characteristic is that it aims at reconciling widely divergent associations. In the past these associations were always suggested by some central idea, openly stated in the
poem; but in modern metaphysical verse, this central idea
may not be stated logically in the poem at all. The poets

believe that the emotional resonance of their images will
be interrupted and deadened by the impact of open statement, and logical structure is replaced by a psychological
process, by a kind of cerebral and emotional shorthand.
Associations leap as indirectly as the knight's move in
chess, the approach to the 'subject' is oblique or peripheral,
and 'meaning' in the usual sense of the word is kept se-
verely in *purdah*. Take, for example, this poem by William Empson:

Note on Local Flora

There is a tree native in Turkestan,
Or further east towards the Tree of Heaven,
Whose hard, cold cones, not being wards to time,
Will leave their mother only for good cause;
Will ripen only in a forest fire;
Wait, to be fathered as was Bacchus once,
Through men's long lives, that image of time's end.
I knew the Phoenix was a vegetable.
So Semele desired her deity
As this in Kew thirsts for the Red Dawn.

The poet, on being asked for an interpretation of this,
called it a 'mild little epigram,' and wrote:

So far as I can see, the thing only means more than
what it claims to say—that is, applies to other things than
this tree in Kew—by a kind of generalisation: I felt that
other people were *like* the tree in Kew.

There may be some obscurity of detail. The tree of
course simply *is* in Kew, and my remarks about it come
from a white label attached to it by the management. The
Tree of Heaven is a translation of a Chinese name for a
tree, one that grows normally in China, and I believe there
is some kind of myth about its magical powers, so this tree
is nearly magical too. Turkestan is cold, China is slow in
growth and unwilling to change its way of life and (so

far as Confucianism goes) rather chilly in its philosophy.
One way or another the countries are supposed to fit the
habits of the tree. The cones of course carry the seeds,
and the tree only casts them in a forest fire, if the white
label is correct. The cones, therefore, only leave their
mother when there is a violent event like the fire at the
end of the world mentioned I think in the Apocalypse,
but anyway a stock medieval idea. The cones are not
wards of time because time does not 'bring them up,' help
them out; they grow up when something like the end of
the world happens, and that is not time but eternity. *That
image* refers back to *forest fire*. Bacchus was born when
Jupiter appeared to Semele in his own nature, as she had
asked him to do, and burnt her up; the forest fire acts
like the father God. Then the Phoenix was also re-born
in a fire, but Phoenix is the scientific name for date-palms
or something like that, so the Phoenix is a vegetable like
the tree. The tree in Kew is unlikely to get a forest fire,
which is what it needs for sexual success, but it may get
one in a Red Dawn—a revolution or a war in which London is so thoroughly burnt that the fire spreads to the
trees in Kew.

Of course you are meant to think of corresponding
human affairs, but you can choose which you like as in
any other description of Nature. Continent passive people
of this sort, with great powers only called out by special
occasions, have got to be admired a great deal, but it
seems rather an absurd kind of dignity, and also it is rather
a dangerous one, because people like that positively enjoy
a big smash-up. The business of not leaving your mother
is made a very undignified one by Freud, and the way
people like this stick to a tradition is rather the same
though it seems dignified. They have a connection with
Bacchus, though they would probably not be interested
in drink, or would disapprove of it, in ordinary life; because they want a big sacred orgy when things smash
up. They are rare and splendid creatures such as the
Phoenix was supposed to be, and able like the Phoenix
to live alone, but this passive power is on the one hand

a dull thing, though helpful, like vegetables, and on the other hand liable to be dangerous, because human beings of this sort generally have a secret desire to make things smash up.

But this chatter on my part doesn't seem necessary to reading the poem. The facts about the tree are surely striking in themselves, and make you feel 'So life's like that, is it?'

§

Nor is all this soldering of complex associations the only difficulty of this type of poetry. The difficulty in Empson is that of intense compression and mental subtlety. But the associations released by each metaphor are profoundly logical. As I. A. Richards has said of him, 'His poetry is metaphysical in the root sense.' Another source of obscurity in present-day poetry, however, arises from the specific *character* of its associations—it arises from the exploitation of the new field of psychological research and the use of associative imagery issuing from the individual subconscious mind.

The extreme statement of this doctrine of 'free association' is linked with the movement known as Surrealism. Surrealism began as a purely literary movement, although subsequent to 1927 its Marxist and political affiliations were emphasized. It was a literary development of the skepticism and defeatism of the Zurich Dadaist exiles. The disillusionment following the war of 1914, and annexations of Freudian psychology, were basic to the Surrealist renunciation of logic. They regarded the logical approach as representative of the scientific and industrial epoch and of spiritual strangulation.

At the outset, André Breton defined Surrealism as 'Pure psychic automatism . . . thought's dictation in the absence of all control exercised by the reason and outside all aesthetic or moral preoccupations.' It was a technique of experience directed primarily not at poetry but rather at the human spirit, which conceives and receives poetry. 'It suggests automatism as a means of winning for man that self-illumination which is needed for his final enfranchisement.'

The Surrealist discipline, indeed, is suggestive of a religious discipline. It consists in the emptying of the human consciousness of all its clutter and jungle of familiar associations in an effort to clear space for the revelation of a transcendent reality. The results, as far as English and American poetry is concerned, have been a series of direct notations of what takes place in the poet's being when preoccupations with logic are reduced to a minimum—a deliberate mining of the veins of imagery buried in the poet's subconscious. A stanza from *The Rites of Hysteria*, by David Gascoyne, will serve as an example:

> In the midst of the flickering sonorous islands
> The islands with liquid gullets full of mistletoe-suffering
> Where untold truths are hidden in fibrous baskets
> And the cold mist of decayed psychologies stifles the sun
> An arrow hastening through the zone of basaltic honey
> An arrow choked by suppressed fidgettings and smokey spasms
> An arrow with lips of cheese was caught by a floating hair

The average reader finds in such poetry simply a series of dream images, a psychological rather than a literary interest. The technique of automatism has no doubt uncovered fields of consciousness which have never before been worked with such thoroughness, and has supplied a fresh sense of visual and physical experience which emerges in many striking associations; but its function seems to be that of mental therapy rather than of artistic creation.

There is a more spiritualized analogy to this procedure in the writings of Eugène Jolas, which have, by his own account, 'an exorcistic function.' Jolas, the editor of *transition*,* is not a member of the Surrealist group, although his poetic theories are remotely related to Surrealism through their common ancestor, the German romantics. His expression of the conflicts within himself issues from a dream state, haunted by figures and objects which 'have no relation to reality'; and since 'traditional language has no vocabulary or syntax for the illogicalities of the dream-state,' he has endeavored to create a new language, a 'sacred Pan-Logos' to communicate his experiences. But the 'anti-poetic' romanticism of the Surrealists and the linguistic mysticism expounded by Eugène Jolas have thus far had little influence on English and American poetry. The Surrealist influence does not appear as an independent 'movement.' It is merged with the whole subject of the intuitive and the irrational elements in poetic creation: a subject which the modern developments in psychology have naturally brought to the fore.

* Wyndham Lewis, in spite of his antipathy to Surrealism, and what he regarded as the 'romantic nihilism' of *transition*, wrote in *The Diabolical Principle* (1931) as follows: '. . . and as to Paris, is it necessary to say that almost all that is good, in formal tendency, or in actual achievement, as either painting or writing (and there is not much) is to be found here and there between the covers of *transition?*'

§

In every age there is a certain shift of focus towards experience which creates new forms of expression, and which makes the reading of new poetry a challenge to accepted conventional standards. Wordsworth was well aware of this when he begged the readers of the *Lyrical Ballads* to be on their guard against 'that most dreadful enemy of our pleasures, our own pre-established codes of decision.' But if the warning was needed in Wordsworth's day, it is needed even more in our own. For our age has faced a more energetic challenge to the old poetic order than that of Wordsworth. Not only has there been a change in the whole mental and emotional coloring of our response to experience, but our knowledge of the actual structure of the mind itself has undergone a revolution.

Thus the problem of both the poet and the reader has been enormously complicated. The consciousness of both has had to adapt itself to new fields of sensibility as well as to new intellectual problems. The effort of the serious poet is to achieve a new synthesis which shall include both. To pursue *only* the exploration of the new fields of subconscious experience (like the Surrealists), or to pursue *only* new mental attitudes (like the communists), is only a partial activity. But the achievement of such a synthesis is prodigiously difficult, hence the unsatisfactory nature of modern poetry.

Since it has always been evident that the inspiration of poetry is very much concerned with the levels of the mind which are inaccessible to common rational experience, it was natural that the new psychological theories of the unconscious should have been eagerly explored by poets. The result has been that just as some of the Victorian poets turned poetry into the handmaid of philosophy, so many of the modern poets have turned her into the handmaid of psychoanalysis. With the conscious and deliberate entry of material drawn from associations private and particular to the personality of the poet, the responses of the reader are clearly required to do a great deal more than they have ever been asked to do before. To each individual writer certain memories from reading or from life become charged with a personal and emotional significance, while they may, perhaps, have no such significance to the rest of the world. The result is that quality of wobbling response which the reader experiences so often in modern verse. The language and the rhythms create a preparation for an unusual and exhilarating poetic experience, but the effect of traveling through it is an alternation of standing upon peaks in Darien and being lost in a labyrinth. As an example of excessive privacy of meaning in poetry, there is a verse in *Perseus* by Louis MacNeice, which runs,

> Shut your eyes,
> There are suns beneath your lids,
> Or look in the looking glass in the end room—
> You will find it full of eyes,
> The ancient smiles of men cut out with scissors and kept
>   in mirrors.

MacNeice, in a recent book of criticism, comments on this:

> To put this more explicitly would disperse the atmosphere of dream. I am describing a mood of terror in

which everything seems to be unreal . . . Such a mood being especially common among children 'the end room' implies a child's fears of long corridors. In such a mood, both when a child and when grown up, I remember looking in mirrors and (a) thinking that my own face looked like a strange face, especially in the eyes, and (b) being fascinated and alarmed by the mysterious gleams of light glancing off the mirror.

This explains the matter; but the associations are purely private affairs of the poet, and it is extremely doubtful if the average reader could arrive at them by any intuition of his own.

§

There is, however, a great deal more of unintelligibility in modern verse than the product of a poet's private symbolism. It is his way of using language in general which defeats the unwary reader. 'Primarily poetry is an exploration of the possibilities of language,' says Michael Roberts, and we must therefore ask ourselves what possibilities of language the modern poets particularly use, and why does the use of them render language so obscure?

Eliot has said in a much quoted dictum that poetry can communicate before it is understood. No one will dispute this; but the question is really to what *degree* it can dispense with 'meaning' in the sense to which we have been accustomed, and still establish clear communication.

We have already said something of the methods by which the modern poet will convey his 'thought,' by means of allusion, symbol or image. We saw how in the opening lines of *Gerontion*, a clear intellectual content was established in the reader's mind without the statement of a 'logical sequence of ideas.' But the full communication of such poetry to the reader depends upon his capacity to sense the implications which lie behind it. If the mental negotiations between the poet and the reader fall through, the 'meaning' remains dumb.

There are readers who are quite content with what they can get from poetry without 'understanding.' They find enough in the communication of sound, fleeting association, mood, suggestion, color, overtones and atmosphere, without any kind of logical or intellectual content. Empson has defined the opposite position in *Seven Types of Ambiguity*. Arguing against the belief that it is enough for the appreciation of poetry to understand the meanings of the words in isolation, he goes on:

It has been deduced from this belief that you are liable to destroy the poem if its meaning is discovered, that it is important to preserve one's innocence about the meaning of verses, that one must use sensibility, and as little intelligence as possible. This is often true, but I take a moral line here, and say it is true only of bad poetry.

It is difficult indeed not to believe that the value of an overtone is its relation to a full tone, and the value of an association is its relation to a central theme. And to say that because the reality of poetry is something very much larger than its rational content, it can therefore dispense with a rational content altogether, is unconvincing. The final use of the works of a watch, however delicate and exquisite in design and craftsmanship, is that when assembled they tell the time. If the dial be omitted, the function of the watch is gravely impaired.

And yet that image is inadequate. The poem should, we may believe, 'tell the time,' but not as a watch-dial does. A dial suggests a statement of scientific precision and accuracy, which is the last thing aimed at or required by the method of poetry. If we want language which is scientifically accurate the proper medium is prose of the kind used for traffic regulation or notices in railway trains. Poetry reveals its truths in language which is supple, pliant and yielding; it works by suggestion, ambiguity and obliquity. There are no rigid confines to its boundaries of 'meaning.' The potentialities of language are its whole width of compass, not only its intellectual aspect, its content of ideas. This intellectual aspect, its common logical basis, is recognized by everyone and is easily communicable to everyone, but what distinguishes poetry from prose is precisely that the poet explores and exploits all the elements beyond that, the elements lurking in the emotional and sensuous values of words. This means all the qualities of beauty, strangeness and power in rhythm and music, texture, color, oddness and subtle collisions. The arguments around obscurity are really arguments as to how far these particular uses of language can *replace* the simple logical values of statement to which we are accustomed.

Eliot, discussing the extreme complexity of the problems of synthesis which face the modern poet in his effort to unify the different planes of his experience, declared that inevitably the poet has to be 'more comprehensive, more allusive, more indirect, in order to force, to dislocate, if necessary, language to his meaning.' He realized that by doing this his 'meaning' would no longer be the expected and familiar one:

> The chief use of the 'meaning' of a poem, in the ordinary sense, may be . . . to satisfy one habit of the reader, to keep his mind diverted and quiet, while the poem does its work upon him: much as the imaginary burglar is always provided with a bit of nice meat for the house-dog. This is a normal situation of which I approve. But the minds of all poets do not work that way: some of them, assuming that there are other minds like their own, become impatient of this 'meaning' which seems superfluous, and perceive possibilities of intensity through its elimination. I am not asserting that this situation is ideal; only that we must write our poetry as we can, and take it as we find it.

Hart Crane pleaded in the same way for this elimination of 'meaning' expressed in logical statement:

> If the poet is to be held completely to the already evolved and exploited sequences of imagery and logic, what field of added consciousness and increased perception . . . can be expected when one has to relatively return to the alphabet every breath or so? In the minds of people who have sensitively read, seen and experienced a great deal, isn't there a terminology something like shorthand as compared to usual description and dialectics, which the artist ought to be right in trusting as a reasonable connective agent toward fresh concepts, more inclusive valuations?

Both the strength and the weakness of the position is shown in *The Waste Land*. The fragmentary, 'dislocated,' formal arrangement reflected very strikingly the sense of disintegration, both personal and social, behind the poem; and the intensity created by the character of the imagery and the rhythm of the verse drove its way into the consciousness of the reader even where the 'meaning' eluded him. He felt that here was a projection of some poignant personal conflict, a drama of inner and outer spiritual disorder which was the work of a deliberate artist, attempting to evoke and present a contemporary consciousness in words, symbols and associations which should communicate its reality without further elucidation (in much the way that modern painters such as Matisse and Picasso and masters such as El Greco and Cézanne have distorted the conventional, representational mode to fit their personal feelings for formal relationships). At the same time the necessity for consulting works of reference to clarify the symbolism, the unfamiliarity of many of the poet's literary associations, the private springs of certain images, and the lack of connectives between the various sets of symbols, all acted as barricades against the storming of the imagination and continue to do so after twenty years of commentary.

§

'We have so built into our nervous systems a demand for intellectual coherence, even in poetry, that we find a difficulty in doing without it,' says I. A. Richards. This is very true. Our early responses to poetry are usually educated on the romantic poets, who seldom transgress logical coherence, and on Shakespeare, who appeals at so many different levels that it is quite easy to ignore those on which he communicates poetic effects in very obscure and difficult language. It is well to remind ourselves again that the problem of the right sort of poetry includes the problem of the right sort of reader.

> If all the good people were clever
> And all clever people were good,
> The world would be better than ever
> We thought that it possibly could;
> But somehow 'tis seldom or never
> The two hit it off as they should,
> The good are so harsh to the clever
> The clever so rude to the good.

In the slight note of exasperation which can be heard in Hart Crane's statement of his position, the voice of the clever is heard addressing the good, and the attitude of the good is hinted at by Coleridge when he declares: 'In all perplexity there is a portion of fear which predisposes the mind to anger.' But it is not only anger which the old-fashioned reader feels towards the obscurity of modern verse. He feels that wide implications towards the whole of life are entangled with these problems of literary practice. He complains of the obscurity on moral and human grounds: he feels that the spiritual and emotional function of poetry in his life has·been denied him by the new cult.

Nobody will deny that he has a case. To stress only the supernormal vision of the poet, to reduce poetry to the effects which can be won from language when its direct qualities of common communication are eliminated, to put all the emphasis on the significance of its obscure and ambiguous elements, is to isolate the poetic activity from all common experience. This is undoubtedly a solution of the poet's dilemma, but it is a negative and partial solution and tends to restrict the poet's audience to the supersensitive 'poet's party.'

The desire for unification and harmony is the ruling spirit of human aspiration in both life and art. Psychoanalysis has given us a picture of the human organism as the battleground of two conflicts: a conflict between conscious and unconscious elements in man's own being, and a conflict between himself and the world in which he lives. The urge which the poet shares with all men to harmonize these conflicts may express itself purely in terms of his art. The poet, particularly in times of social disintegration such as the present, may withdraw from any attempt to contemplate the reality of the external world, and concentrate upon giving formal verbal outline to his personal *response* to the problem of living. The discipline of creation is itself a rigid exercise in the achievement of psychic equilibrium. If he achieves it·by poetic means which satisfy himself it will be a matter of no importance to him whether he communicates freely with his fellows. But the poet who feels also the compulsion to relate himself organically with the external world, who includes both the reality of that world and the reality of his own consciousness in the material he aims to synthesize, must inevitably find some method of communication which appeals not only to a partial and limited activity of the human potential, but to the whole of it. Since the poet is an artist in language, he will inevitably use language in its intuitive and symbolic and ambiguous aspects as well as in its direct and intellectual ones, but he will—indeed, he must—use language through which he can appeal to the common human nature of his audience. It will be the whole being of the poet which participates in his act of creation, and the whole being of the reader which responds.

CHAPTER 5

The Nineteen Thirties

> The lesson of our time is sore:
> Having and to have no more,
> Within the smoky reference
> Of life and its indifference.
> CHARLES MADGE. *Ode*

> . . . a low dishonest decade:
> W. H. AUDEN. *September 1, 1939*

> What was said by Marx, boys?
> What did he perpend?
> No good being sparks, boys, waiting for the end.
> Treason of the clerks, boys,
> Curtains that descend,
> Lights becoming dark, boys, waiting for the end.
> WILLIAM EMPSON. *Just a Smack at Auden*

THE real revolutionary movement in twentieth century poetry is that embodied in the early work of T. S. Eliot and the Pound of *Hugh Selwyn Mauberley*. As Gertrude Stein says in her book on Picasso:

Complications are always easy but another vision than that of all the world is very rare. That is why geniuses are rare, to complicate things in a new way that is easy, but to see things in a new way that is really difficult, everything prevents one, habits, schools, daily life, reason, necessities of daily life, indolence, everything prevents one, in fact there are very few geniuses in the world.

In the early poems of Eliot and Pound we do get a new vision, a new revelation, as significant in its own way as

95

that which Wordsworth and Coleridge brought to the world in 1798. It followed the usual course of literary movements which are rooted in profound changes in society and the individual, and not merely in literary fashion. That is, it was first ridiculed and reviled by established authority, and then when the poets had become recognized by the public—which means when the public had recognized itself in the poets—they were widely imitated, and all sorts of further 'complications' developed within the new vision. Just as Keats and Shelley followed Wordsworth and Coleridge, so Auden and Spender followed Eliot and Pound. And just as Keats wrote—with irritation unusual in him—'I will have no more of Wordsworth. . . . Why should we be owls when we can be eagles?' and just as Shelley published *Peter Bell the Third*, so in 1938 we find Auden writing: 'There have been experimental writers to whom we owe much, but to whose real deficiencies we owe nothing: they live in Italian towns . . . and in vestries among the camphor and the offertory bags.' He is writing of 'poetic isolation,' and he declares the end of it has come:

The only justified retreat is a loneliness from which everything and everybody is more visible, the loneliness in the centre and not on the edge. Unless a poet can be there sometimes at least, he has no right to exist and no claim to be tolerated and need expect no good man to listen to him.

Such a declaration seems on the face of it to be a heartening symptom of the recuperation of poetry from its decline into individual dilettantism, and of a hope that it may play a more robust and stimulating part in contem-

porary civilization. It seems a prelude to the poetry we
spoke of in the last chapter, the poetry which should
merge the fresh areas of sensibility disclosed by psychological investigation, with some fresh exploration of the
external world; a poetry which should not only record
the *response* of the individual mind to the problems of
living, but should create some affirmative attitude towards
the problems of life. The watchword of the nineteen
twenties had been 'transition'; perhaps the nineteen thirties would arrive.

But there is a significant remark in Wyndham Lewis'
Blasting and Bombardiering which might be put beside
the criticisms of Auden. Of Eliot, Pound, Joyce, himself,
and the group of artistic revolutionaries of the twenties,
Lewis writes:

We are not only 'the last men of an epoch' . . . we are
more than that. . . . *We are the first men of a Future
that has not materialized.* We belong to a 'great age' that
has not 'come off.' We moved too quickly for the world.
We set too sharp a pace. And, more and more exhausted
by War, Slump, and Revolution, the world has *fallen
back.*

He believes that any artistic effort on the grand scale is
now impossible. 'Martial law conditions have come to
stop. The gentler things of life are at an end.'

However, the fact that gentler things were doomed
would not perturb the poets of the early nineteen thirties,
for they were busy dedicating themselves not to artistic,
but to political revolution. Notable among American left-
wing poets are Horace Gregory, Muriel Rukeyser, Kenneth Fearing, Kenneth Patchen and Delmore Schwartz,

but the so-called Auden-Spender group of Marxist poets was the strongest influence during the first half of the decade. They dictated the fashion, and it came to be considered intellectually a trifle dowdy if verse did not wear red.

§

> *This is the way the world ends*
> *Not with a bang but a whimper.*

When this group of young writers came to the fore in the early thirties it seemed at the outset as if the whimper was to be changed to a bang. In place of the evocative, indecisive rhythms of the early twenties came provocative, challenging cadences with quite new intonations. The hollow men whispering together in meaningless dried voices were transformed into a generation with ringing, sometimes rude young tones whose meaning was unmistakable. There was Hugh MacDiarmid, somewhat older than the others, discarding the Scots Doric to shout,

> The Christians have had two thousand years
>   And what have they done?
> Made the bloodiest and beastliest world
>   Under the sun.

And Auden's ghoulish Witnesses smacking their apocalyptic chops over the imminent collapse of the bourgeoisie:

>   you'll have a fall
> We've been watching you over the garden wall
>   for hours,
> The sky is darkening like a stain,
> Something is going to fall like rain
>   and it won't be flowers.

Rex Warner is even more explicit:

Now all together sing All Power,
not tomorrow but now in this hour. All Power
to Lovers of Life, to Workers, to the Hammer, the
Sickle, the Blood—

Eliot's poetry had embodied a deep spiritual disgust at the ugliness and emptiness of the modern world. But in his early poems his attitude was a negative one. His drama was an inner conflict, a drama of the soul, waged in the individual human spirit. And it was a drama without any conclusion. The conflict upon which the young Marxists embarked was very different. It was a materialist and humanitarian revolt. In the midst of a world of industrial collapse, of cold furnaces, of poverty in the midst of plenty, they described the horrors of the present and sang with determined hearts of the glories of the future. Auden pictures the scene and challenges the effete ruling classes in a vigorous reproduction of the rhythms of *Locksley Hall*:

Shut up talking, charming in the best suits to be had in
town.
Lecturing on navigation while the ship is going down.

Drop those priggish ways for ever, stop behaving like a
stone;
Throw the bath-chairs right away, and learn to leave
ourselves alone.

If we really want to live, we'd better start at once to try;
If we don't, it doesn't matter, but we'd better start to die.

Day Lewis calls in more melodious tones:

You that love England, who have an ear for her music,
The slow movement of clouds in benediction,

Clear arias of light thrilling over her uplands,
Over the clouds of summer sustained peacefully:
Ceaseless the leaves counterpoint in a west wind lively,
Blossom and river rippling loveliest allegro,
And the storms of wood, strings, bass, at year's finale:
Listen. Can you not hear the entrance of a new theme?

The new theme was that of a dedicated life. As Spender declared: 'The writer who grasps anything of the Marxist theory feels that he is moving in a world of reality and in a purposive world.' There is no longer room for individual isolation:

private stars fade in the blood-red dawn
Where two worlds strive.

The note of aspiration, dumb since the emotional glamour of the war sonnets of Rupert Brooke, sounds again, 'blowing out of the sunrise.' The poems of these young men are filled with exhortations to action, to raise a wind which shall shake the world out of its sleepy sickness, to show 'the springlike resources of the tiger,' to meditate on the known and unknown heroisms of those 'who were truly great.'

§

The mood was short-lived; perhaps because it sounded somewhat hollow in a cause where deeds and not words stir the imagination most deeply. For the most part this generation of young poets, a few years before so sure of 'the palpable and obvious love of man for man,' and of the dawn which was to

explode like a shell
Around us, dazing us with light like snow,

now escape into political romanticism by writing popular journalism about Spain or China, or escape into the individual romanticism of the solar plexus by variations on the theme 'our sex and our sorrows are ever about us.' The general emotional coloring of the late thirties is one of gloom and hopelessness. To read any of the yearly anthologies of the period is to hear a melody on the triangle of Time, Despair and Frustration, or to listen to changes rung upon the bells of death. George Barker in *Elegy No. 1* concludes:

> Lovers on Sunday in the rear seats of cinemas
> Kiss deep and dark, for is it the last kiss?
> Children sailing on swings in municipal parks
> Swing high into the reach of the sky,
> Leave, leave the sad star that is about to die.
> Laugh, my comedians, who may not laugh again—
>   Soon, soon,
> Soon Jeremiah Job will be walking among men.

Auden turned from the energetic propaganda of the fine choruses in *The Dog Beneath the Skin* to gruesome satiric ballads like *Miss Gee*, or gloomy advice to 'Go down with your world that has had its day'; and MacNeice, waiting for the deluge, skirled his sardonic lament on the Bagpipe:

> It's no go my honey love, it's no go my poppet;
> Work your hands from day to day, the winds will blow
>   the profit.
> The glass is falling hour by hour, the glass will fall for
>   ever,
> But if you break the bloody glass you won't hold up the
>   weather.

The gloomy objective landscape is matched by an even gloomier subjective one. The enthusiastic Boy Scout spirit of general uplift, all the good will and misty idealism which the young poets would have ridiculed if they had met it in Tennyson or Longfellow, is replaced by nostalgic longings for certainty and serenity; litanies of doubt, incantations of loneliness and fear, the death wish, images of prisoners, cages, bars; the ever-present knowledge that 'the worm curls about the bone's splinter.' It all makes us suspect that 'the masses' were little more than a symbol to objectify personal moods of individual magnanimity or unrest. There is little now to distinguish red from any other emotional coloring. 'A common greyness silvers everything,' a common incapacity to come to grips with the enemy, a craving for any sort of faith which would supply a personal harmony.

> . . . fretful even in leisure
> I fidget for different values,
> Restless as a gull and haunted
> By a hankering after Atlantis.

Prokosch, in America, has the same longings as MacNeice, and the same disillusionments:

> We think of a paradise, we think of a heaven,
> Cataracts flashing, fruit on all the trees,
> The cliffs yielding their gold, wings over seas,
> Songs in whose web our simple hearts lie woven:
>
> But from this childhood's heaven issues forth
> In his black cloak the hooded shape of man,
> And overhead no laden boughs, no suns,
> But storms, gulls, comets flung from a dark north.

Spender longs

> to find release
> From the continual headache
> And the necessity for such long journeys;

The necessity of being alone
And the never being alone
Away from the lighted cities of the brain.

It all has a dying fall. We are left with a picture of man haunted by loss and disappointment, weakened by the struggle with circumstance and spiritual disharmony, sure only of one thing, that he is neither the master of his fate nor the captain of his soul.

§

Many of these young poets are skilled metrists and craftsmen, who write most melodious, complex and highly fashioned verse. The most compelling individual voice is that of Auden, but though it maintains versatility and variety of tone, its volume and resonance seem to diminish rather than to increase. Mr. Gladstone once made a speech in which he described Egypt as 'the almost certain egg of a great empire,' and Auden's friends have the same faith in him:

We salute in Auden . . . the first English poet for many years who is a poet all the way round. There are angles from which Mr Eliot seems a ghost and Mr Yeats a gleam. . . . But Auden does live in a new day. He is solid enough, poke him where you will, not crumbling like fudge. He is traditional, revolutionary, energetic, inquisitive, critical and intelligent.*

He is all these things, and yet we may try to distinguish between the greatness he was born with and has achieved, and that which has been thrust upon him. He differs from almost all contemporary poets in being original, lively,

* Geoffrey Grigson.

and copious in invention and experiment: he can storm the sense and stir the mind, with a careless prodigality of talent conspicuous among the careful poetic exercises of many of his contemporaries.

He has every gift, in fact, except that which he most commends, that of being at the center from which everything and everybody is more visible. That surely implies a steadier vision, a more coherent consciousness, a greater tenacity of purpose, than Auden's poetry reflects. Yet he is again unlike his contemporaries in having gleams of the real moral passion which a great poet never lacks. In his early prayer for 'power and light' and 'a change of heart,' beginning 'Sir, no man's enemy . . .'; in his simple address,

> O love, the interest itself in thoughtless Heaven,
> Make simpler daily the beating of man's heart;

in passages in *The Ascent of F6;* in some of his sonnets on China, there is a rare directness and searchingness of feeling and expression. As an individual poem illustrating this capacity for deep seriousness without solemnity, *Voltaire at Ferney* is a good example:

Voltaire at Ferney *

Perfectly happy now, he looked at his estate:
An exile mending watches glanced up as he passed,
And went on working; where a hospital was rising fast,
A joiner touched his cap; an agent came to tell
Some of the trees he'd planted were progressing well.
The white alps glittered. It was summer. He was very
    great.

* This version of the poem appeared in *The Listener* of March 9, 1939.

Far off in Paris where his enemies
Whispered that he was wicked, in an upright chair
A blind old woman longed for death and letters: he would
    write
'Nothing is better than life.' But was it? Yes, the fight
Against the false and the unfair
Was always worth it. So was gardening. Civilise.

Cajoling, scolding, scheming, cleverest of them all,
He'd led the other children in a holy war
Against the infamous grown-ups; and like a child been sly
And humble when there was occasion for
The two-faced answer or the plain protective lie,
But, patient as a peasant, waited for their fall:

And never doubted, like D'Alembert, he would win.
Only Pascal was a great enemy; the rest
Were rats already poisoned; there was much, though, to
    be done,
And only himself to count upon;
Dear Diderot was dull but did his best;
Rousseau, he'd always known, would blubber and give in

Night fell, and made him think of women. Lust
Was one of the great teachers; Pascal was a fool.
How Emilie had loved astronomy and bed;
Pimpette had loved him too, like scandal; he was glad.
He'd done his share of weeping for Jerusalem; as a rule,
It was the pleasure-haters who became unjust.

Yet, like a sentinel, he could not sleep: the night was full
    of wrong,
Earthquakes and executions. Soon he would be dead,
And still all over Europe stood the horrible nurses,
Itching to boil their children: only his verses,
Perhaps, could stop them; he must go on writing. Over-
    head
The uncomplaining stars composed their lucid song.

Auden creates a complex and individual world. He has
a most variegated consciousness, in which symbols of

health and disease, communism, the Oedipus complex, 'Nanny,' school life, 'the private nocturnal terror,' economics, and 'the frontier' (which includes frontiers of time, of psychological experience, and of class), all pervaded sometimes by emotion, sometimes by wit, blend to create an unmistakable atmosphere peculiar to himself. But though these various strains blend, they do not cohere. He projects no comprehensive vision which is large enough to include them all. Auden's satire is often very good fun, but it is concerned almost entirely with externals: it is superficial and crude. To be effective, satire must spring not from negative but from positive standards of value. It must be sure of itself or it becomes the aggressiveness which is a defense against a sense of personal insecurity. It must not only diagnose sickness, it must envisage health.

Auden still gives the impression of a splintered personality unsure of itself, and lacking fundamental convictions —that element which gives direction and permanence to the Eliot of *Ash Wednesday*, to D. H. Lawrence or Yeats, or to smaller poets like Frost and Marianne Moore. It is the quality which in the last century belonged in different ways to Wordsworth, Keats, Shelley and Browning, but which Byron lacked. Auden's admiration for Byron is significant. He has some of the same cynical wit, the same hatred of shams, the same patches of genuine feeling and enthusiasm—those updraughts of the spirit which whirl him out of 'the malady of the quotidien'—the same streaks of irresponsibility and bad taste, the same fertility and iridescence, the same lack of centrality and reserve power.

§

It is no doubt helpful to a poet to hold a political faith which gives him a feeling that 'he is moving in a world of reality and in a purposive world.' But at the same time it is quite unnatural for a poet to find any political creed enough for his needs. As Empson says: *

To produce a pure proletarian work of art the artist must be at one with the worker; this is impossible, not for political reasons, but because the artist is never at one with the public.

If the poet had not an organism more sensitive than that of the public he would not be a poet. It may happen, of course, that a poet's political convictions are fundamental to his work, as Milton's were; but we do not have that feeling about many modern poets. There are more who are like the girl in William Saroyan's story who refused to let the communist make love to her because the masses were sure to come into it and she preferred it private. But the poet cannot easily escape his age and its overwhelming preoccupations. George Barker, writing of this problem, says:

I do not so much mean that the poet nowadays can write only about the poor. But what I do mean is that the poet cannot now escape the poor without betraying his nature as a poet; any more than he can escape the possibility of catastrophe by war without betraying his nature as intelligent. Both of these matters exist, and dictate the angle of glance at reality. About both the poet as well as other people must endeavour to act.

* *English Pastoral Poetry.*

The strain imposed upon the sensitive individual by this feeling of compulsion is very apparent in the poets of to-day. Spender, for instance, is tortured by it. He is by nature a poet of introspection and sensitive psychic notation; and his efforts to 'take action' in his later poetry, to write objectively about poverty and war, lack challenge and incisiveness.

Louis MacNeice too is at odds with his time, but he makes no attempt to take 'action' in his poetry. He expresses the attitude of a large number of people who want only to live intelligent cultured lives in comfortable surroundings, and who feel wistfully, if sardonically, plaintive that they have been born into an era when this is so difficult to do:

> All that I would like to be is human, having a share
> In a civilized, articulate and well-adjusted
> Community where the mind is given its due
> And the body is not distrusted.

In a series of skillful, nostalgic lyrics MacNeice has created this elegiac mood. He finds it impossible to hold any single-minded faith, and remains 'incorrigibly plural' in interests, though at the same time he realizes that such tastes render him 'obsolete.' He would keep out the real world if he could; he would try and stay Time by turning it into the deathless immobility of Art—forming a Poussin fête in the mind from the actuality of the passing hour:

> While the lawn-mower sings moving up and down
> Spirting its little fountain of vivid green,
> I, like Poussin, make a still-bound fête of us
> Suspending every noise, of insect or machine.

Garlands at a set angle that do not slip
Theatrically (and as if for ever) grace
You and me and the stone god in the garden
And Time who also is shown with a stone face.

But all this is a dilettante's lie.
Time's face is not stone nor still his wings,
Our mind, being dead, wishes to have time die
For we being ghosts cannot catch hold of things.

Such poetry as that of Spender and MacNeice has a
vogue at the moment, for it finds an echo in the feelings
of a vast number of what Eliot calls 'decent godless people.' It is the poetry of 'the intolerable neural itch,' and
though it avoids the simplification which makes Marxist
poetry so vaporous, it has a brittleness of surface which
impairs the effectiveness of its irony. There is no doubt
something to be said for the view that the abnormally sensitive consciousness has much to contribute to the community. We may agree with Auden up to a point when
he declares:

I hate the modern trick, to tell the truth,
    Of straightening out the kinks in the young mind,
Our passion for the tender plant of youth,
    Our hatred for all weeds of any kind.
    Slogans are bad: the best that I can find
Is this: 'Let every child have that's in our care
As much neurosis as the child can bear.

Goddess of bossy underlings, Normality!
    What murders are committed in thy name! . . .

But although much good poetry has been made out of
an oversensitive nervous system, maladjustment is not necessarily the same thing as inspiration, more especially if

it is an imitated attitude of maladjustment, or at least one strongly colored by a prevailing fashion. The poet who has something important to say will find his own way of saying it, whatever his environment, as the history of poetry amply proves. In this decade the most striking example is Dylan Thomas.

§

Dylan Thomas writes directly from the rich treasury of Christian and Celtic tradition, spinning this heritage into a vital human symbolism. He utilizes such common human experiences as birth, growth, love, marriage, religion and death, giving their expression new shapes in images of air, light, water, earth and blood. In his poem *From Love's First Fever to Her Plague* the growth of man from infancy to maturity is analyzed in terms of evolution from the simple singular vision of childhood to the crowded complexity of mature experience. From the time when

> All world was one, one windy nothing,
> My world was christened in a stream of milk.
> And earth and sky were as one airy hill,
> The sun and moon shed one white light.

through the periods of childhood and adolescence

> The body prospered, teeth in the marrowed gums,
> The growing bones, the rumour of manseed
> Within the hallowed gland, blood blessed the heart,
> And the four winds, that had long blown as one,
> Shone in my ears the light of sound,
> Called in my eyes the sound of light.

to the knowledge of maturity gradually revealed

I learnt the verbs of will, and had my secret;
The code of night tapped on my tongue;
What had been one was many sounding minded.

None of the younger poets of today is closer to physical life in the biological sense and to spiritual life in the
religious sense than Dylan Thomas in the poetry he has
thus far published. In *Before I Knocked and Let Flesh
Enter* these interests are united in describing Christ's
agony of prescience within the womb of His mother:

> As yet ungotten, I did suffer;
> The rack of dreams my lily bones
> Did twist into a living cipher,
> And flesh was snipped to cross the lines
> Of gallow crosses on the liver
> And brambles in the wringing brains.

The entire poem is composed with a reverent familiarity
rarely found in modern poetry, but common to folk-
poetry in the Christian tradition. Thomas' religious expression lacks the sensitive asceticism of Hopkins. Its
coarse, homely directness reflects the ruder piety of
common men:

> My Jack of Christ born thorny on the tree?

It is the common man that concerns Thomas in his
poetry. Man living, loving, using his five senses and functioning fully. 'Man be my metaphor,' he has said. And
his luminous imaginative vision has penetrated those mysteries of human existence which deny him direct knowledge. He speaks for the child in the womb:

> If my bunched, monkey coming is cruel.
> Rage me back to the making house. My hand unravel
> When you sew the deep door. The bed is a cross place.

Bend, if my journey ache, direction like an arc or make
A limp and riderless shape to leap nine thinning months.

and answers for the mother with equal feeling:

No. Not for Christ's dazzling bed
Or a nacreous sleep among soft particles and charms
My dear would I change my tears or your iron head.
Thrust, my daughter or son, to escape, there is none,
    none, none,
Nor when all ponderous heaven's host of waters breaks.*

Thomas is an illustration of the truth that if a poet of today is to achieve an expression rooted in direct living and containing the seeds of permanence, he must do more than reflect the situation of the sensitive, intelligent individual in an uncongenial environment. He must seek to ally himself with forces which are timeless and universal. We shall see something of this task and how some modern artists have accomplished it, in the following chapters.

* From the poem entitled *If My Head Hurt a Hair's Foot.*

CHAPTER 6

Poets of Affirmation

D. H. LAWRENCE

> Let the reader recall, going back a little way into
> history, the gallery of talents—poets, thinkers, jour-
> nalists, talkers—especially favoured by Society. How
> many minds, described as "fins," "delicats," "ai-
> mables," "pleins de grace" he will find: but how few
> minds to which "*vigoureux*" could be applied.
>
> JULIEN BENDA

'NOW in literature, the elements with which the creative power works are ideas current at the time. And I say *current* at the time, not merely accessible at the time; for creative literary genius does not principally show itself in discovering new ideas, that is rather the business of the philosopher. The grand work of literary genius is a work of synthesis and exposition, not of analysis and discovery; its gift lies in the faculty of being happily inspired by a certain intellectual and spiritual atmosphere, by a certain order of ideas, when it finds itself in them. . . . But it must have the atmosphere; it must find itself amidst the order of ideas, in order to work freely; and these it is not so easy to command. That is why great literary epochs are so rare; that is why there is so much that is unsatisfactory in the productions of many men of real genius.'

No one could call our age one of the great creative epochs, and one reason for it is suggested in this passage

113

from Arnold, though the argument has to be pushed further. Arnold did not regard his own age as a great creative epoch, though we are inclined to disagree with him. The fact that it had no specific intellectual and spiritual center appeared to him to be a weakness. He regarded the various individual manifestations of faith such as those of Newman, Carlyle, Ruskin and George Eliot as illustrations of an unsatisfactory state of cultural activity. And being a man of sensitive rather than vigorous temperament himself, and wedded to the ideal of the classics as the fixed standard of judgment, he was inclined to underestimate and distrust a general imaginative fecundity—the simple abounding creative gusto of such writers as Dickens, Thackeray and Browning.

But our own age is certainly in much worse case. It is not that there are not spiritual and intellectual ideas *current* in great force today, but that they are not ideas with which the modern artistic spirit can ally itself easily. The spiritual and intellectual *vitality* of the present world is directed into the channels of active military, political or economic reorganization on rigid totalitarian lines, and the values of the modern artist are not in step with that vitality. In earlier ages of the world the poet found no difficulty in identifying himself wholeheartedly with the spirit of aggressive militarism, and in exalting warfare as good in itself and the leader of men to battle as the finest example of the hero. Even as late as Elizabethan days Marlowe could put his whole heart into creating *Tamburlaine*, or Shakespeare his in *Henry V*. But neither the communist, the fascist nor the Nazi ideal has produced an intellectual or spiritual atmosphere which has 'happily inspired' a distinguished company of poets.

The difficulty of the serious poet in contemporary circumstances is obvious. If he cannot identify himself with any of the current ideologies, he must either accept some framework of traditional belief within which his individual temperament can find satisfaction, or forge a personal faith or despair from the 'accessible' ideas around him and his own total consciousness. And he must do this without any of the general vital and national afflatus around him which the Victorian mentality enjoyed.

§

There has, presumably, never been so great a break with tradition in poetry as during the last twenty years. Even that of the Renaissance is not comparable. That was an expansion and growth, aided by an unparalleled dynamism of the human spirit, but it was a blossoming which fed itself from the roots of the past quite as much as from the air and sunshine of the present. The contemporary situation is quite different: for not only have the dogmatic religious beliefs of an earlier age lost much of their force, but there has been a drying up of other sources of spiritual nourishment. The loss of touch with the elemental realities of the earth, which an ever-increasing urbanization of life inevitably brings; the decay of the imaginative value of the myth, and of the myth-making faculty; and what might be called the flight from reason, have all contributed to the emotional and intellectual poverty of the present. Cut off from traditional channels of communication with these universal values of a great past, the modern poet is left with a meager spiritual equipment—the psychology of the unconscious, the Marxian dialectic and a sense of frustration.

The result is reflected in our contemporary poetic situation. It is most obvious in the overwhelming preponderance of the personal lyric. The difficulty of a writer in an age of unstable faith is to find an inclusive attitude. The poetry of the present age has been mainly that of mood and temperament, unrelated to any larger coherence. It is clear that a single emotional impulse is much more easily controlled and focused than a larger and more complex integration of impulses. Such integration demands a more elaborate verse form, or the evidence of organic growth which can emerge only in a substantial corpus of work. And in most of those who are of years to have achieved this, it is not there. What is there is a hatred of existing outer and inner *dis*order, and a continual notation of the distress which the poet suffers in an uncongenial environment. He reveals a personality, but not a personality which is reflected in any coherent and inclusive pattern of response to existence. And as Eliot has said, 'the first requisite usually held up by the promoters of personality is that a man should "be himself"; and this "sincerity" is considered more important than that the self in question should, socially and spiritually be a good or a bad one.'

This 'personal heresy' has given us a great deal of distinguished minor verse, but a sense of exile from the tradition and wisdom of the race, and of existence in an alien contemporary environment, is ultimately a negative and sterile condition. It is natural, therefore, that the poetry which we believe will prove to be the most enduring of the age will be that of those poets who have achieved an organic fusion of individual with universal values.

§

Man's struggle with Destiny, his sense of his own active consciousness existing in a universe controlled by a power greater than himself, is the recurring pattern of experience woven into living and into literature. The necessity of the assertion of the individual, and the necessity of the submission of the individual to a larger scheme, are the central problems of all government, personal and social. Within that framework the emotional and intellectual life of mankind, with its innumerable variations of racial and temporal patterns, and the innumerable moods, longings, revulsions of the human body, mind and spirit, works itself out. It is behind and beyond all differences of personality and of epoch, expressed in new forms by new minds in all ages, the ultimate irony informing every vision of man's tragedy, the ultimate harmony informing every vision of his triumph.

But this basic pattern finds new symbolic interpretation in the terms of different civilizations and different temperaments. The tragic hero—the projection of man's active sense of his own existence, and of the desire to impose the shape of his own values upon that existence, with inevitable personal failure and the final absorption of his own effort into a more powerful design—appears in one age as Oedipus, in another as Hamlet, in another as Samson, in another as Peer Gynt. The quest of the individual soul to find nourishment and sustenance from forces beyond itself and finally to fulfill itself in harmony with the universe it inhabits, is symbolized now in the wanderings of Ulysses or of Aeneas, now in the structure of the *Divine Comedy*, or of *Paradise Lost* or of Shelley's *Prometheus Unbound*. The question of our 'belief' in these symbols does not involve acceptance of the mythology or the theology or the philosophy in whose terms the vision may be projected, and which for the individual poet represents a satisfying medium for its communication. The poetic truth of such visions is that they continue to give imaginative expression to certain profound and unchanging experiences of reality, which have been re-lived and re-affirmed by succeeding generations.

And it is in the continuity of such traditional comprehensive human experiences that there has been so conspicuous a gap in our own age. The nineteenth century world produced two great attempts: *Prometheus Unbound* and *The Dynasts* (although the latter was not published until 1904). Shelley restated a Greek myth in the spirit of his own ethic. Hardy, in *The Dynasts*, projected the general drama of the Napoleonic wars, and the particular conflicts of individual relationships, within a comprehensive philosophic framework. This allowed him to objectify a vision of universal values, giving an impressive critical commentary on the affairs of men. The whole is a great architectonic of the imagination, a great modern myth of the problems of human will and consciousness.

But neither in poetry nor in prose have we had anything comparable since. We have no modern myths, creating traditional experience in modern metaphors, as it were, uniting the experience of the community with the individual sensibility of the artist, linking fact and fancy, the contemporary and the eternal in the popular imagination, and providing a new basis for some wide common ground of reference and symbol.

In the place of any such comprehensive vision we find that certain persistent experiences of the human spirit have had particular expression in poetry today, and it is significant that they are the instincts fostered by a sense of frustration. There is the desire to regress to the safe dependence of the world of childhood, the world ruled by 'Nanny'—a mood created in fine poetic terms in D. H. Lawrence's *Piano;* or the craving for the dark warmth and comfort of the womb, the prenatal unconscious; or the death wish—that instinct to attain ultimate freedom, not by seeking roots that can clutch even in the stony rubbish of modern civilization, but by slipping into that last peace, that final release from tension and conflict beyond even foetal or childish dependence. This does not, of course, mean that the poetry creating these attitudes is necessarily inert or feeble. Such attitudes can be given the most actively realized poetic expression, as they are, for instance, in some of the poetry of Hart Crane. But the only integrated visions of universal quality have been the personal phantasmagorias of *The Waste Land* and Joyce's *Ulysses,* works born out of the new twentieth century consciousness of the world of the personal subconscious, works in which the controlling power is the ordering force in art, not the ordering force in life.

§

The subjection of the reason, with its corollary, the revolt against law, from which much of our general modern impasse springs, has had various sources in the thought of the present age. The Bergsonian insistence on the *élan vital*, on instinct and intuition as the revelation of truth; the theory of the psychologists that reason is dominated by desire, and can only function within those limits; the Marxist emphasis that the quality of a man's manhood depends not on himself but on his economic environment; the Nazi dependence on a particular blood-stream as the repository of wisdom; all these have undermined the older view that a man's reasoning faculties gave him such controlling power as he possessed in the universe.

And the poet who first affirmed this revolt, with all the force of a great if misshapen genius, was D. H. Lawrence.

§

Not I, not I, but the wind that blows through me!
A fine wind is blowing the new direction of Time!
If only I let it bear me, carry me, if only it carry me!
If only I am sensitive, subtle, oh, delicate, a winged gift!
If only, most lovely of all, I yield myself and am borrowed
By the fine, fine wind that takes its course through the chaos of the world
Like a fine, an exquisite chisel, a wedge-blade inserted;
If only I am keen and hard like the sheer tip of a wedge
Driven by invisible blows,
The rock will split, we shall come at the wonder, we shall find the Hesperides.

Oh, for the wonder that bubbles into my soul,
I would be a good fountain, a good well-head,
Would blur no whisper, spoil no expression.

Any attempt to make an ordered and consistent philosophy from the work of Lawrence is an impossibility.
There have been few successful attempts to rule as an
autonomous monarch without a constitution, and Lawrence too failed. He was always the victim of his own
contradictory moods, and he expressed them all in poetic
form. As a result a great deal of his verse is what someone
has described as 'a case-book of immediate emotions.' He
was always more interested in himself and his thesis than
in the technique of his poetry. He is frequently repetitive and turgid; he often blurs his whisper and spoils his
expression. The question, To let go or to hold on, baffled
him. Shall man let go, identify himself with 'some vast
revolutions of creative chaos,' be willing to lose himself,
to let himself slip

    like weed, like eggs of fishes,
  like sperm of whales, like germs of the great dead past
  into which the creative future shall blow strange un-
        known forms,

or shall he hold on to his humanity,

                          brace himself up
  and lift his face and set his breast
  and go forth to change the world?

This dilemma gave Lawrence's work, as it gave his life,
a central instability, a kind of desperate insecurity which
made his tone often aggressive and overemphatic. But the
main reason for the impossibility of rationalizing Lawrence

is that you cannot rationalize ecstasy, and his convictions were fundamentally a *mystique* which was fluid and formless, though continually fed afresh from the quenchless vitality in himself. 'I am a passionately religious man,' he says, and again, 'I am essentially a fighter,' and those are the two fundamental qualities in his nature.

It would be difficult to find two men more utterly unlike than he and Eliot, yet it is the awareness of the spiritual drought parching contemporary civilization which provided the inspiration of both, and some of the deepest experiences of each follow the same psychological pattern, though they are projected in seemingly contradictory symbols.

Vitally the human race is dying. It is like a great uprooted tree, with its roots in the air. We must plant ourselves again in the universe. . . . We are bleeding at the roots, because we are cut off from the earth and sun and stars.

Like all sensitive individualities, Lawrence revolts passionately against the spiritual deadness which paralyzes society,

All the people that go with the fittings and furnishings, the upholstered dead that sit in deep armchairs;

against the tyranny of the machine, the 'money muck' which has diseased humanity, all the emptiness and heartlessness of industrialism. He has alternate moods of choking rage and hatred for 'the rabbit-blood of the myriads'—

> Stand up, stand up for justice
> ye swindled little blokes!

and profound pity for the helpless slaves of the machine:

For oh the poor people, that are flesh of my flesh,
when I see the iron hooked into their faces
their poor, their fearful faces,
I scream in my soul for I know that I cannot
take the hook out of their faces . . .
nor cut the invisible wires of steel that pull them
back and forth, to work,
back and forth to work,
like fearful and corpse-like fishes hooked and being played
by some malignant fisherman on an unseen shore . . .

But he sees no hope whatever in political revolt. 'I get
more and more revolutionary every minute, but for *life's*
sake'; 'one must speak for life and growth amid all this
mass of destruction and disintegration.' The only evil is
to deny life, he says, and his message always comes back
to that. His faith is in the potentialities of man to evolve
something splendid out of a renewed chaos, but he sees
no hope of amelioration in mankind as it is. He wants to
rend and deracinate the past and the present, and to im-
plant in mankind a new technique of living:

I realize that the greatest thing the world has seen is
Christianity . . . but I count Christianity as one of the
great historical factors, the has-been. . . . There is something beyond the past. . . . Unless for us the future takes
place, we are death only. . . . I find my deepest desire to
be a wish for pure unadulterated relationship with the
universe, for truth in being.

This ache for 'being' he regards as the ultimate hunger.
It is the urge to create a new tree of life from the roots
already within us. And to satisfy it, to find his real food,
man must sink 'personality'—'this horror of little swarm-
ing selves'—and base his relationship with his fellows on
purpose; not upon what we *are*, but upon what we wish

to bring to pass. But this elimination of the self must not be accomplished in any spirit of suppression or abnegation of earthly desires, which, to Lawrence, is to deny life. Man must seek his consummation beyond himself, in union with some universal life-force, greater than any merely human activity, but which man can touch and transmit.

Lawrence sees that the only lonely and personal thing in man is his mind, and therefore he hates the mind as the great stumbling block to the new life of complete emotional spontaneity. The mind is the great enemy of the 'blood,' injecting poison into the veins, meddling officiously with the naïve, physical consciousness, interrupting the free communion of the soul with God, the source of creative life, by emphasizing the importance and value of the self.

§

There is a curious parallelism between Lawrence's description of the central experience of his faith and that of other writers on religious experience—including Eliot himself. The central theme to Lawrence is the experience of Death and Rebirth, which is the core of so much of the myth and religion of the world. 'Do not be sad,' he writes to a friend whom he believes to be sharing his own struggles. 'It is one life which is passing away from us, one "I" is dying, but there is another coming into being. . . . Don't be afraid, don't doubt it, it is so.' And in *New Heaven and Earth* he describes his own change.

I was so weary of the world
I was so sick of it,
everything was tainted with myself,

skies, trees, flowers, birds, water,
people, houses, streets, vehicles, machines,
work, recreation, governing, anarchy,
it was all tainted with myself.

. . . .

At last came death, sufficiency of death,
And that at last relieved me, I died.

. . . .

God, but it is good to have died and been trodden
    out . . .
absolutely to nothing. . . .
For when it is quite, quite nothing, then it is everything.
When I am trodden quite out, quite, quite out,
every vestige gone, then I am here
risen, accomplishing a resurrection,
risen, not born again, but risen, body the same as before,
new beyond knowledge of newness, alive beyond
    life. . . .

In all ages mystical experience has made use of sexual
symbolism for the idea of union with the divine, and of
the phases of extinction and resurrection which accompany it; but with Lawrence, in the early stages of his
belief, it was the actual experience of a perfect sexual
union which released him from slavery to one form of
consciousness and gave him his freedom. The importance
of the true sexual union to him was the discovery through
it that man must go out of himself to touch the sources of
creative power: it released him from the earlier torment
of his dependence on his mother, and from the intrusion
of similar feelings in his relations with other women:

She is all not-me, ultimately.
It is that that one comes to.
A curious agony, and a relief, when I touch that which is
    not me in any sense . . .

It is the major part of being, this having surpassed oneself
this having touched the edge of beyond, and perished, yet
    not perished.

It is the same experience, in different psychological terms,
as the second poem in *Ash Wednesday*. Lawrence uses
sex as the symbol of the unsingleness of the individual, the
impossibility of self-withdrawal, the narrow fulfillment
of Self within the self:

Sex, which breaks up our integrity, our single inviolability,
    our deep silence,
Tearing a cry from us . . .
Torn, to become whole again, after long seeking for what
    is lost,
The same cry from the tortoise as from Christ, the Osiris-
    cry of abandonment,
That which is whole, torn asunder,
That which is in part, finding its whole again throughout
    the universe.

This conception Lawrence afterwards presented in a
contemporary situation in *Lady Chatterley's Lover*, but
his despair of modern civilization drove him to seek
further symbols of what he was trying to express in
the rituals of primitive cultures, in the worship of the
'dark Gods' who are 'a source of rest and unspeakable
renewal,' the world of *The Plumed Serpent*. There he
found 'the phallic reality,' the experience which he describes characteristically elsewhere as

    the exquisite orgasm of coition
With the godhead of energy that cannot tell lies.

At the end of his life, Lawrence's conception of the
phallic consciousness lost its early violence and stridency,

and his *Last Poems*, written in the shadow of death, flow into the rhythms of 'an inward and lovely peace.' He had finished with the conflict.

> Is life strife, is it a long combat?
> Yes, it is true. I fight all the time.
> I am forced to.
> Yet I am not interested in fight, in strife, in combat,
> I am only involved.

In those last months he accepted his isolation and welcomed it, alone with the feel of 'the living cosmos softly rocking,' soothing, restoring and healing:

> I know no greater delight than the sheer delight of being
>   alone.
> It makes me realize the delicious pleasure of the moon
> that she has in travelling by herself: throughout time,
> or the splendid growing of an ash-tree
> alone, on a hill-side in the north, humming in the wind.

Nor is his philosophy of 'darkness' ever given such beautiful expression as in *Bavarian Gentians*.

> Reach me a gentian, give me a torch
> let me guide myself with the blue, forked torch of this
>   flower
> down the darker and darker stairs, where blue is dark-
>   ened on blueness,
> even where Persephone goes, just now, from the frosted
>   September
> to the sightless realm where darkness is awake upon the
>   dark
> and Persephone herself is but a voice
> or a darkness invisible enfolded in the deeper dark
> of the arms Plutonic, and pierced with the passion of
>   dense gloom,
> among the splendour of torches of darkness, shedding
>   darkness on the lost bride and her groom.

Finally even images of life and love leave him, and in *Song of Death* he sings only of the 'most lovely lapsing' of the soul as it sweeps round 'the great final bend of unbroken dark.'

§

It was the tragedy of Lawrence that he could never relate himself in any real way with his own world: 'The world is as it is. I am as I am. We don't fit very well.' He could form no real human relationships: nothing 'comes through' to him from other people, he declares bitterly. 'What ails me is the absolute frustration of my primeval societal instinct. . . . I think societal instinct much deeper than sex instinct, and societal repression much more devastating.' Like all prophets, he wanted leadership because he was convinced that what he had to say was the Truth, and that it would save the world: 'I have inside me a sort of answer to the *want* of today'; but the world would not listen, or if it did, it misunderstood him. We find him making continual efforts to form a community of kinship in belief, seeing himself in imagination perhaps as a Buddha sitting under a bo-tree teaching his disciples; always convinced that it is the artificiality of modern life which blocked the way, and not his own temperament; always hoping that some new place would provide the satisfactory answer to his needs, wandering about the globe trying to escape from his own daemon, and calling it Europe or Asia or America or Australia. Finally crying out that he feels he will go mad because there is nowhere to go, no new world; and finally dying, as he says, of chagrin because of his complete isolation, but still asserting,

> You tell me I am wrong.
> Who are you, who is anybody to tell me I am wrong.
> I am not wrong.

Like Eliot, or the communists, he is intolerant of any belief other than his own, and he can be extraordinarily offensive in his expression of it: 'I've got a nice canvas of sun-fauns and sea-nymphs laughing at the Crucifixion.' He had no real sympathy with any of his fellow writers and quarreled sooner or later with all his friends. Lady Caroline Lamb, in one of her frequent arguments with her husband, produced that useful piece of abstract reasoning, 'Truth is what one believes at the moment,' and Lawrence could be equally dogmatic on the subject of inconvenient facts which contradicted his own convictions. Aldous Huxley describes how he attempted once to argue with him on a matter of scientific truth, and Lawrence replied to his objections, 'I don't care about evidence. . . . I don't feel it *here*,' and pressed his two hands over his solar plexus. 'One should stick by one's soul and by nothing else,' he declares, but he had no sympathy with others who followed the same precept, and his own soul was so frequently divided against itself that he could find no lasting peace.

§

Ye elemental Genii, who have homes
  From Man's high mind even to the central stone
Of sullen lead; from heaven's star-fretted domes
  To the dull weed some sea-worm battens on . . .

cried Shelley; but Lawrence's daemon had no such scope. His weakness as a leader was the very narrow limitation of his logos. Like all religious teachers, he knew the solution of human problems to lie in the merging of the individual into something greater than himself, but he felt this life-force to be purely animistic, with no relation to either intellectual or moral vitality. He refused to accept the fact that man feels more than the beasts because he thinks more, or that the value of any experience is not merely in its intensity, but in its comprehensiveness. He did not care about order: 'I don't mind a chaos, if I feel sometimes the wind blows through the chaos.' A flame, he declares, is not a flame because it lights up two and twenty objects on a table, it is a flame because it is *itself* and the only important matter is that we have forgotten ourselves. But the light is still there.

> There is a swanlike flame that curls round the centre of
>   space
> and flutters at the core of the atom
> there is a spiral flame-tip that can lick our little atoms into
>   fusion
> so we roar up like bonfires of vitality,
> and fuse in a broad hard flame of many men in a oneness.

This social fusion Lawrence quite failed to accomplish, and his solution of a return to primitive cultures was a regressive instinct providing an escape from contemporary problems rather than a cure for them; but there is triumphant proof in his own work that man could be a bonfire of vitality. He hated people who enjoyed what they called the flavor of his personality, 'as if I were a cake or a wine or a pudding'; but Lawrence will live because of the unique strange world of bright and intense

consciousness he created, because in his writing we touch
a *way of feeling* entirely unlike anyone else's, and have
something of its glowing vigor and its 'delicate and snail-
horn perception of beauty' communicated to us.

> This sea will never die, neither will it ever grow old
> nor cease to be blue, nor in the dawn
> cease to lift up its hills
> and let the slim black ship of Dionysos come sailing in
> with grapevines up the mast, and dolphins leaping.

There is no more exquisite and startling descriptive
poet: from the sheer vividness of the turkey.

Your wattles are the colour of steel-slag which has been
    red-hot
And is going cold,
Cooling to a powdery, pale-oxydised sky-blue,

and his sudden demonic onrush,

> All the bronze gloss of all his myriad petals
> Each one apart and instant . . .
> So delicate:
> Yet the bronze wind-bell suddenly clashing . . .

to the tenderness of the cyclamen,

> Waking, pricking their ears
> Like delicate very young greyhound bitches
> Half yawning at the open, inexpressed
> Vista of day
> Folding back their soundless petalled ears.

He can always find the inevitable visual image, whether
it is the drooping Victorian shoulders of the kangaroo,
or the she-goat 'smiling with goaty munch-mouth, Mona
Lisa,' standing with her long-tangled sides like an old rug
thrown over a fence.

But this descriptive power is an external quality. It is

in his power to live *into* experience that Lawrence is unique. His peculiar voice and vision are unmistakable:

> In the northern hemisphere
> Life seems to leap at the air, or skim under the wind
> Like stags on rocky ground, or pawing horses, or springy
>   scut-tailed rabbits.
>
> Or else rush horizontal to charge at the sky's horizon,
> Like bulls or bison or wild pig.
>
> Or slip like water slippery towards its ends. . . .

Life seems to live in some specially fervent and enhanced way in all he wrote; he spent his life experiencing living with a never-ending sense of wonder. Even dying and death are a new marvel:

> snatches of lovely oblivion, and snatches of renewal,
> odd, wintry flowers upon the withered stem, yet new,
>   strange flowers
> such as my life has not brought forth before, new blos-
>   soms of me.
>
> then I must know that still
> I am in the hands of the unknown God
> he is breaking me down to his own oblivion
> to send me forth on a new morning, a new man.

We feel that he went forth every morning a new man, to partake of new life. 'For man, the vast marvel is to be alive . . . a part of the living incarnate cosmos. I am a part of the sun as my eye is part of me. That I am a part of the earth my feet know perfectly and my blood is a part of the sea.' It was this apocalypse—exactly the same vision as that of the seventeenth century Christian mystic Thomas Traherne: 'You never enjoy the world aright till the sea itself floweth in your veins, till you are clothed with the heavens and crowned with the stars'—that Lawrence struggled to reveal to his contemporaries in those rough, undisciplined, repetitive, but always urgent and disturbing rhythms of his.

Flowers and Men

Flowers achieve their own floweriness and it is a miracle.
Men don't achieve their own manhood, alas, oh alas! alas!

All I want of you, men and women,
all I want of you
is that you shall achieve your beauty
as the flowers do.

Oh leave off saying I want you to be savages.
Tell me, is the gentian savage, at the top of its coarse stem?
Oh what in you can answer to this blueness? . . .
Tell me! tell me! is there in you a beauty to compare
to the honeysuckle at evening now
pouring out his breath?

T. S. ELIOT

Love has her priests in the poets, and sometimes
you will hear a voice which knows how to hold her
in honour: but not a word will you hear about faith.
Who is there who can speak in honour of this
passion?

S. KIERKEGAARD. *Fear and Trembling*

The Waste Land is built upon an idea common to fertility ritual and Grail legend—the fundamental conception of death and rebirth evidenced alike in the rhythms of nature and in Christ's resurrection from the dead. The troubled questioning note on which the poem ends is not devoid of hope. The arid plain is *behind* the speaker as he meditates.

> Shall I at least set my lands in order?

But there is no substantial promise of hope, no assurance that the thirst for the waters of faith and healing will be assuaged. There is not even the *sound* of water in that 'decayed hole among the mountains.' The empty chapel has 'no windows and the door swings.' Man is 'fear in a handful of dust.'

The Hollow Men (1925) might be described as an epilogue to *The Waste Land*. It is a meditation preliminary to the retreat and purgation of *Ash Wednesday*. In the form of five variations its theme is that of spiritual degradation. The epigraph, 'A penny for the Old Guy,' is a phrase used by children who disguise themselves, and displaying a stuffed effigy of Guy Fawkes, collect pennies for fireworks on the fifth of November. The opening section of the poem seems to say: It is we, the representatives of lifeless contemporary religion, who are the straw-men. Religion, as we practice it, is

> Shape without form, shade without colour,
> Paralyzed force, gesture without motion;

We shall not be remembered even as men whose spiritual energies have followed the wrong path, but only as futile empty men.

> Those who have crossed
> With direct eyes, to death's other Kingdom

> Remember us—if at all—not as lost
> Violent souls, but only
> As the hollow men
> The stuffed men.

The second section recalls Dante's dream of Beatrice's eyes in the Purgatorio—the symbol of spiritual vision. 'Death's dream kingdom' is the state of death-in-life which is Eliot's conception of the world today. In this nightmare world, the hollow man who is speaking dares not face the realities of spiritual experience. Any gleams he has of it are sentimentalized into vague, fragmentary, fitful images; 'sunlight on a broken column,' a tree singing, voices in the wind's singing, a fading star. He knows that his vision is unreal and a self-deception, but he cherishes it. He will even disguise his real self in order to maintain it, and to avoid the challenge of positive faith.

The third and fourth sections describe the sterility and frustration of his attitude. The tortured question,

> Is it like this
> In death's other kingdom
> Waking alone
> At the hour when we are
> Trembling with tenderness . . .

—that is, is the life after actual death like this?—discloses his hidden craving for spiritual assurance. But this can be satisfied only by those who pass through this life, 'death's twilight kingdom,' with 'direct eyes.' Life at best is

> this brief transit where the dreams cross
> The dreamcrossed twilight between birth and dying
> *Ash Wednesday vi.*

But the dreams can be only the empty hopes and unreal
fantasies of blind men groping together,

unless
The eyes reappear
As the perpetual star
Multifoliate rose

Unless the darkness can be lit by the windows of the spirit.

The childish singsong which opens the fifth section
suggests the nursery stage of make-believe which has transformed Guy Fawkes, a 'lost violent soul' into a stuffed
'guy.' But the 'prickly pear' recalls the 'cactus land' of section three, and the adult implications behind that change.
The attitude of religious 'make-believe,' of meaningless
formal ritual and emotional fantasy, blights all hope of
spiritual growth. The typography here bears a significance
in the thought-pattern. The interfering Shadow is cast
upon action by the attitude expressed in the marginal
phrases. It is the attitude of inactive Christianity which
rejects positive spiritual life in favor of temporal interests,
relegating the spiritual to the world to come, with the
added evasion, 'life is very long.' There is no virtue, nor
passion, nor violence in such an attitude. It is the final
whimper of a world degraded in spirit.

In 1931 Eliot made a more explicit plea for active faith
when he wrote in *Thoughts After Lambeth:*

The World is trying the experiment of attempting to
form a civilized but non-Christian mentality. The experiment will fail; but we must be very patient in awaiting
its collapse; meanwhile redeeming the time: so that the
Faith may be preserved alive through the dark ages before us; to renew and rebuild civilization, and save the
World from suicide.

It is the theme of 'redeeming the time' which characterizes the bulk of Eliot's work from *Ash Wednesday* * onward. His devotional poetry marks the beginning of a new spiritual experience.

The note of humility so evident in the earlier poems such as *Prufrock*, *Gerontion* and *The Waste Land* becomes an actively penitential mood in Eliot's later work. Spiritual discipline, purgation of guilt, and redemption are the key concepts of the devotional attitude in *Ash Wednesday*, *Murder in the Cathedral* and *The Family Reunion*. They are also the basis of Eliot's intellectual experience of Christianity. In *The Idea of a Christian Society* he has written:

. . . one can assert that the only possibility of control and balance is a religious control and balance; that the only hopeful course for a society which would thrive and continue its creative activity in the arts of civilization is to become Christian. That prospect involves, at least, discipline, inconvenience and discomfort; but here as hereafter, the alternative to hell is purgatory.

But the disciplinarian and purgatorial element in Eliot's doctrine of redemption does not function passively. As we have indicated in our interpretation of *The Hollow Men*, Eliot advocates an activist Christianity. The suffering envisaged in a spiritual discipline is action, and the action is suffering, and both are within the pattern of the Eternal Will.

                              acting is suffering
    And suffering is action. Neither does the actor suffer

* For an analytic interpretation of *Ash Wednesday* the reader is referred to an article by Leonard Unger in *The Southern Review* (Spring 1939).

Nor the patient act. But both are fixed
In an eternal action, an eternal patience
To which all must consent that it may be willed
And which all must suffer that they may will it,
That the pattern may subsist, for the pattern is the action
And the suffering, that the wheel may turn and still
Be forever still.

The action and the suffering are subordinated to the eternal pattern which is itself movement in stillness.

Eternal pattern is the theme of *Burnt Norton*. Reflections of Eliot's intellectual thesis in this poem also appear in the texture of *Murder in the Cathedral* and *The Family Reunion*. A key to *Burnt Norton* is suggested by the epigraph reference to Heraclitus of Ephesus. Heraclitus declared that everything was continually changing and chose fire as a symbol of perpetual flux. The primordial fire symbolized that divine rational process, the harmony of which constitutes the law of the universe. For Heraclitus the law of Reason Universal was the logos and virtue consisted in a subordination of the individual to universal reason. Christian thought expanded the logos of Heraclitus into the personified Logos, the Word, combining a redemptive function with an aesthetic ordering of the universe. The central motif of *Burnt Norton* depends on this latter concept and an interplay of the philosophies of flux and permanence.

The concept of the eternal presence of all time is introduced in the opening lines. In form of expression this section moves sharply from dry philosophical statement to a warmer imagery of example. The conclusion reached is that the weakness of humankind requires the illusion of time broken into a sequence of past, present and future.

The eternal presence of the past would rob us of our sentimental reflections on 'what might have been' and 'what has been' by making such considerations purposeless. 'Dust' becomes a symbol of the past, while the hidden laughing 'children' symbolize the future. The coexistence of past, present and future points to the eternal pattern or Logos.

> Go, go, go, said the bird: humankind
> Cannot bear very much reality.
> Time past and time future
> What might have been and what has been
> Point to one end, which is always present.

The second section opens with a compact series of images suggesting the power of reconciliation exercised by the eternal pattern over the apparently irreconcilable oppositions in the visible universe:

> Below, the boarhound and the boar
> Pursue their pattern as before
> But reconciled among the stars.

The rhythms then lengthen, the structure becomes more tenuous and the language thins into abstraction to describe the stable and enduring form beyond the change our senses witness. But again the closing lines conclude that mankind in its weakness cherishes memories which can exist only in the illusion of 'time':

> But only in time can the moment in the rose-garden,
> The moment in the arbour where the rain beat,
> The moment in the draughty church at smokefall
> Be remembered; involved with past and future.

The third section presents a contrasting picture of the miserable dimness of the time-world (the world of dedication to temporal interests). There is neither light (the Word) to give it form, nor darkness (asceticism) to purify the soul. It is a 'twittering,' twilight world. The second part of this section describes the purifying experience of 'the dark night.' The only other way to redemption lies in an abstention from temporal interest,

> . . . while the world moves
> In appetency, on its metalled ways
> Of time past and time future.

The short fourth section is a rhythmic arrangement of simple lyrical images. Our temporal interests have covered the spiritual light. The movements in nature testify to a love of light. The light is in the Logos, 'At the still point of the turning world.'

The fifth section describes the eternal pattern of the Logos:

> Only by the form, the pattern,
> Can words or music reach
> The stillness, as a Chinese jar still
> Moves perpetually in its stillness.
> Not the stillness of the violin, while the note lasts,
> Not that only, but the co-existence,
> Or say that the end precedes the beginning,
> And the end and the beginning were always there
> Before the beginning and after the end.
> And all is always now.

The stillness in movement of eternal form is contrasted with the movement of details in the pattern. The final lines recapitulate the coexistence of past, present and future in the eternal pattern.

§

In his early poetry Eliot's method contained much objective as well as subjective dramatic expression. Character, atmosphere and décor were frequently constructed with an almost theatrical calculation of effect. Prufrock's problem, *The Portrait of a Lady*, and the cockney last-minute gossip in *The Waste Land* are as emphatically the dramatist's reproduction of reality as they are the poet's translation of reality into the idiom of imagination. But with the inward turn of his vision in *Ash Wednesday* Eliot's poetry lost its exterior drama and became purely subjective. A liturgical symbolism replaced the realism of his earlier work and the poet's conflict with the outside world was submerged in a spiritual conflict within himself. The relationship between his inner conflict and the outside world is reflected in the poetry, but being at one remove from the conflict itself the relationship with external reality loses its dramatic impact. It is a conflict of beliefs and concepts within one man's soul, and not the external dramatic embodiment of beliefs and concepts. In view of Eliot's natural bent towards dramatic expression it is not surprising that he should attempt to objectify his spiritual conflict in a more dramatic form.

The form taken by Eliot's turn to the theater appears to be connected with his religious preoccupation in a more general way. There is at least a hint of this in *A Dialogue on Dramatic Poetry* (1928), where the following 'interesting theory' is proposed:

I have a suggestion to put forward. It is this: can we not take it that the form of the drama must vary from age to age in accordance with religious assumptions of the age? That is, that drama represents a relation of the human needs and satisfactions to the religious needs and satisfactions which the age provides. When the age has a set religious practice and belief, then the drama can and should tend towards realism, I say *towards*, I do not say arrive at. The more definite the religious and ethical principles, the more freely the drama can move towards what is now called photography. The more fluid, the more chaotic the religious and ethical beliefs, the more the drama must tend in the direction of liturgy. Thus there would be some constant relation between drama and the religion of the time. The movement, in the time of Dryden, and indeed of Corneille, and indeed of Aristotle, was towards freedom. Perhaps our movement should be towards what we called, in touching upon the ballet, form.

Of the two plays, *Murder in the Cathedral* and *The Family Reunion*, the former is the more successful both in dramatic structure and in the adjustment of Eliot's poetic expression to the exigencies of dramatic form. The tone of the play is set by the somber choral mood which dominates the action from beginning to end. Solemn and brooding, the language of the chorus is packed with a peculiarly vital energy of metaphor:

> We have not been happy, my Lord, we have not been
> too happy.
> We are not ignorant women, we know what we must
> expect and not expect.
> We know of oppression and torture,
> We know of extortion and violence,
> Destitution, disease,
> The old without fire in winter,
> The child without milk in summer,
> Our labour taken away from us,
> Our sins made heavier upon us.
> We have seen the young man mutilated,

The torn girl trembling by the mill-stream.
And meanwhile we have gone on living,
Living and partly living,
Picking together the pieces,
Gathering faggots at nightfall,
Building a partial shelter,
For sleeping, and eating and drinking and laughter.

The entire passage introduced by these lines is an excellent example of the intensified dramatic effect created by variations in the underlying pattern of music and metaphor. The vivid direct language of the opening lines quoted above is supported by a repetitive monotone cadence. It is a straightforward, dispassionate report of common incident in the life of these simple women. With the second section of this passage, however, a note of spiritual misgiving is introduced and the 'new terror' infects both language and rhythm:

God gave us always some reason, some hope; but now a
    new terror has soiled us, which none can avert, none
    can avoid, flowing under our feet and over the sky;
Under doors and down chimneys, flowing in at the ear
    and the mouth and the eye.
God is leaving us, God is leaving us, more pang, more
    pain, than birth or death.
Sweet and cloying through the dark air
Falls the stifling scent of despair;
The forms take shape in the dark air:
Puss-purr of leopard, footfall of padding bear,
Palm-pat of nodding ape, square hyaena waiting
For laughter, laughter, laughter. The Lords of Hell are
    here.

The tone has changed from resignation to foreboding, and the language becomes a pattern of sinister metaphor. The supporting rhythm takes on a swift irregular move-

ment arresting ear and eye with sharp rhyme at points
of emphasis and significant pause.

In contrast to the physical energy of the choral metaphor, Eliot has written the Archbishop's part in an austere intellectual idiom. Even the colorful vision of remembered sensuous experience reflects Becket's intellect
in its fastidious arrangement of image:

> Delight in sense, in learning and in thought,
> Music and philosophy, curiosity,
> The purple bullfinch in the lilac tree,
> The tiltyard skill, the strategy of chess,
> Love in the garden, singing to the instrument,
> Were all things equally desirable.

This dramatic contrast of expression is maintained on each
side of the play's central point—the interpolated Christmas
sermon. At this point Becket and the chorus are united
in the simplicity and fervor of these gently reasoned
words of spiritual solace.

The weakness of *The Family Reunion*, on the other
hand, is that at its best it is a poem and at its worst remains
an undramatic play. Between these two extremes there
are occasional moments of dramatic excitement in which
the action and the poetry share the same spirit and move
on the same plane. Agatha is the vital element of the play.
Without her presence and lines the poetry flags and the
play relaxes into recitation. Her scenes and exchanges
with Harry are brilliant, persuasive dramatizations of abstraction, an experiment rarely undertaken in modern
playwriting. And in the scenes between Agatha and Harry
there is an ease of execution indicating a sympathy felt by
Eliot for this material.

There are hours when there seems to be no past or
    future,
Only a present moment of pointed light
When you want to burn. When you stretch out your
    hand
To the flames. They only come once,
Thank God, that kind. Perhaps there is another kind,
I believe, across a whole Thibet of broken stones
That lie, fang up, a lifetime's march. I have believed this.

It is the tempo of emotional speech warmed within a
deeply felt human problem, and dramatically far more
compelling than the ill-adjusted realism of such lines as

I might have known you'd throw that up against me.
I know I wasn't one of your favourite students:
I only saw you as a hard headmistress.
Who knew the way of dominating timid girls.
I don't see you any differently now;
But I really wish that I'd taken your advice
And tried for a fellowship, seven years ago.

Realism of this kind must be sparingly and delicately employed where strict spiritual conflict speaks through a
poetic structure. Eliot's problem in this play has been
chiefly one of language and its adjustment to a theme
which shifts continually between realism and the world
of the spirit. The play conveys the feeling of an experimental search for a medium which will accommodate both
levels with as little compromise as possible. In the direct
dramatic incidents such as take place between Agatha and
Harry the adjustment is achieved and the relentless concentric movement of the play is felt in the urgency and
note of resignation in their language. The speeches of
Agatha with Harry form a dramatic pattern of actual
human need and sympathy, whereas the indirect drama of

gossip, conference, scheme and commentary established
by the other characters, singly and in chorus, contributes
nothing to the progress of the play. With the possible
exception of Amy, the minor characters are responsible
for a waste of words which so shatter the dramatic structure that the Agatha-Harry speeches cease to function as
dramatic elements and stand as isolated poems pursuing
into deeper places the philosophic mood of *Burnt Norton:*

> Time past and time future
> What might have been and what has been
> Point to one end, which is always present.

We find its echoes in Harry's agonized logic:

> Oh, is there any difference!
> How can we be concerned with the past
> And not with the future? or with the future
> And not with the past?

and the symbols of rose-garden, bird and 'unseen eye-
beam' pass from *Burnt Norton* into Agatha's vision of the
sorrow she has known:

> I only looked through the little door
> When the sun was shining on the rose-garden:
> And heard in the distance tiny voices
> And then a black raven flew over.
> And then I was only my own feet walking
> Away, down a concrete corridor
> In a dead air. Only feet walking
> And sharp heels scraping. Over and under
> Echo and noise of feet.
> I was only the feet, and the eye
> Seeing the feet: the unwinking eye
> Fixing the movement. Over and under.

Such passages are dramatic not because their subject is
dramatic but because they are contrived in a highly sug-

gestive excitement of language. Sound combines with meaning to produce vivid action within a small vision, a microscopic drama of abstractions. The larger scene, on the other hand, the play in its totality of action, speech and character is static and comes to life only at those occasional points of successful adjustment of language to two planes of human existence. But its life at these points is that of dramatic poetry and not of poetic drama. For the movement of these passages is outward from within, whereas the truly dramatic moves inward from without. The movement of drama is from the world of Thebes or Elsinore to the world within one man's soul, and not the reverse movement. The movement of the *Oresteia* itself is inward from a world of war and lust and vengeance, and its action is the unmistakable action of flight without rest. The movement of *The Family Reunion* is outward from a troubled conscience to the world of reality in Wishwood, where the need of expiation finally becomes manifest. The smaller drama of abstractions dominates the play because of the superior quality of its poetic expression. The result of this superiority, however, is a fatal disproportion of dramatic interest between the play as a whole and its parts.

Eliot's poetic sympathies in recent years have turned more and more to dry, reflective abstraction and a finely whittled symbology and concept, and away from the plenty and phantasmagoric procession of *The Waste Land*. As *Burnt Norton* proves, this is suitable poetic material in the hands of such a skillful and sensitive technician. But whether it will support the more varied and involved movement of drama still remains to be seen.

W. B. YEATS

> . . . the phantasmagoria through which I can alone
> express my convictions about the world.
>   Preface to *The Wild Swans at Coole*

IN AN essay on *Poetry and Tradition* Yeats defines Style
as 'high breeding in words and argument.' He continues:

> In life courtesy and self-possession, and in the arts
> style, are the sensible impressions of the free mind, for
> both arise out of the deliberate shaping of all things, and
> from never being swept away, whatever the emotion,
> into confusion and dulness.

There is no better description of Yeats' peculiar and
particular quality of writing. He was always the most
deliberate and conscious of artists, holding no delusions
about poetry's being the spontaneous overflow of powerful feelings, but knowing that it was a craft, a 'sedentary
toil,' which exhausted the artist as much as it delighted
him:

> The fascination of what's difficult
> Has dried the sap out of my veins, and rent
> Spontaneous joy and natural content
> Out of my heart.

His technique finally reaches that almost insolent ease,
freedom and strength which is the result of the perfect
control of his medium; his rhythms have the flexibility,

tautness, precision and muscular mastery of the great dancer. But though the language of his maturity is the idiom and syntax of our common heritage of speech, it has always that stamp of personal nobility and seemingly effortless authority for which no better summing-up could be found than to call it 'high breeding in words and argument.'

In width of scope he far exceeds any of his contemporaries. He is the only poet since the eighteenth century who has been a public man in his own country and the only poet since Milton who has been a public man at a time when his country was involved in a struggle for political liberty. This may not seem an important matter, but it is a question whether the actual kind of life lived by poets for the last two hundred years or so has not been one great reason for the drift of poetry away from the life of the community as a whole, and the loss of touch with tradition. Once the life of contemplation has been divorced from the life of action, or from real knowledge of men of action, something is lost which it is difficult to define, but which leaves poetry enfeebled and incomplete. Yeats responded with all his heart as a young man to the reality and the romance of Ireland's struggle, 'all that delirium of the brave.' He saw that 'a terrible beauty' is born among all these men and women, resigning their parts in 'the casual comedy' and united in a living purpose. He can perfectly understand the simple heroic leader who cries,

> O plain as plain can be
> There's nothing but our own red blood
> Can make a right Rose Tree.

He lived to be completely disillusioned about the value of
the Irish rebellion. He saw his dreams of liberty blotted
out in horror by 'the innumerable clanging wings that
have put out the moon,' and comments with sardonic
bitterness,

> Now days are dragon-ridden, the nightmare
> Rides upon sleep: a drunken soldiery
> Can leave the mother, murdered at her door,
> To crawl in her own blood, and go scot-free;
> The night can sweat with terror as before
> We pieced out thoughts into philosophy,
> And planned to bring the world under a rule,
> Who are but weasels fighting in a hole.
>
> . . . .
>
> We who seven years ago
> Talked of honour and of truth,
> Shriek with pleasure if we show
> The weasel's twist, the weasel's tooth.*

It brought him to the final conclusion of the futility of
all discipline that is not of the whole being, and of 'how
base at moments of excitement are minds without culture': but he remained a man to whom the life of action
always meant something very real. Even in the civil war,
as he meditates on the failure of the movement, and his
own withdrawal from it into poetry, he feels the pull
towards life among the fellowship of men:

> I turn away and shut the door, and on the stair
> Wonder how many times I could have proved my worth
> In something that all others understand and share. . . .

He stills his 'ambitious heart' with the knowledge that

* *Nineteen Hundred and Nineteen.*

>   the abstract joy,
> The half-read wisdom of daemonic images
> Suffice,

but he gloried always with a real fellow feeling in the
Irish patriots who combined vigor of mind with vigor
of body and the joy of positive life:

> But stories that live longest
> Are sung above a glass;
> And Parnell loved his country
> And Parnell loved a lass.

And he loved 'those careless old writers one imagines
squabbling over a mistress, or riding on a journey, or
drinking round a tavern fire, busy and active men.' When
old age came, he cried out in horror at it.

> What shall I do with this absurdity—
> O heart, O troubled heart—this caricature,
> Decrepit age that has been tied to me
> As to a dog's tail? *

He prayed that he might not become 'a wise old man, that
can be praised of all,' but remain 'a foolish passionate man,'
and even when his body finally craved rest, his spirit
hated to admit the inevitable individual human defeat.
His 'old man's eagle mind' remained untamed and un-
daunted.

> Grant me an old man's frenzy,
> Myself I must remake
> Till I am Timon and Lear
> Or that William Blake
> Who beat upon the wall
> Till Truth obeyed his call.†

* *The Tower.*
† *An Acre of Grass.*

Had Yeats had any real dramatic genius he would have found in the drama the complete artistic expression for the totality of his vigorous mind and personality. As it is he created it into lyric verse of the richest and most varied range, from mystic, and often misty, abstract profundity to homely pungency; from the most highly wrought magnificence of patterned language to gnomic epigram or dramatic ballad or pure love lyric.

§

No young contemporary poet can find it harder than Yeats found it to be a poet,

> thrown upon this filthy modern tide
> And by its formless, spawning, fury wrecked;

alive in a world which has lost two of the three types of men whom he thinks have made all beautiful things—the aristocrats, who have made beautiful manners, 'the unperturbed and courtly images,' and the countrymen, who have made beautiful stories and beliefs. There is only the third left, the artists, who have made all the rest. And how be an artist, a poet, in a civilization which has lost all stability and all direction?

> Turning and turning in the widening gyre
> The falcon cannot hear the falconer;
> Things fall apart; the centre cannot hold;
> Mere anarchy is loosed upon the world,
> The blood-dimmed tide is loosed, and everywhere
> The ceremony of innocence is drowned;
> The best lack all conviction, while the worst
> Are full of passionate intensity.*

* *The Second Coming.*

The early Yeats turned his back on this world and escaped into the tapestry land of legend, being convinced that 'all great poets have wrought their poetry out of the dreams that were dreamed before men became so buried in their individual destinies and trades, that every man grew limited and fragmentary.' * But he found that this withdrawal rendered the poet also limited and fragmentary; he became 'unemphatic and spiritual,' and he was driven to the search for some vision which should relate the world of imagination and the world of actuality, the dream and the reality, the abstract and the concrete.

To find this the poet, like all creators, must work out in the solitude of his own mind the patterns he will project upon the blank page of the future. In a late poem, *The Long-Legged Fly*, Yeats embodies, in a series of concrete pictures, a vision of the working of the great creative forces of the universe. He sees these as order, love and art. 'Like a long-legged fly upon the stream,' the mind of the organizer, the lover, the artist, 'moves upon silence.' All are concerned with the search for a rhythm, a pattern, an ordering, which must be imposed upon the formless living of life. And such forms and rhythms were Yeats' own all-absorbing quest.

§

In the Preface to *Prometheus Unbound*, Shelley states that

poetical abstractions are beautiful and new, not because the portions of which they are composed had no previous existence in the mind of man or in nature, but because the

* *Literary Ideals in Ireland.*

whole produced by their combination has some intelligible and beautiful analogy with those sources of emotion and thought, and with the contemporary condition of them.

Yeats found himself faced with the difficulty of all modern poets—the lack of an accepted religious and cultural heritage which should provide both a groundwork of communication between poet and audience, and a groundwork of belief in which his own intelligence should find liberty of movement. Where Lawrence evolved his doctrine of animistic ecstasy and Eliot found satisfaction in Anglican Christianity, Yeats based a philosophy on what is commonly spoken of as 'magic,' but which is more properly a doctrine of symbolism.

He has described in *A Vision* how his wife proved to have powers as a medium, and how the system of philosophic thought contained in the book was revealed through messages received by her in a condition of trance, and transcribed by himself. The basis of this occult metaphysic is the idea of the Unity of Being, symbolized in the figure of the Great Wheel, or of the twenty-eight phases of the moon, which correspond to the complete history of the soul. The whole course of civilization, and of every individual personality, can be calculated within the geometrical designs of cones, gyres and spheres, and described in terms of primary and antithetical, objective and subjective, urges; of lunar and solar tinctures, and of the four faculties of what he calls Will, Mask, Creative Mind and Body of Fate. But though Yeats at one time hoped that the system would prove a revelation of truth satisfying alike to his mind and spirit, it did not prove so. Through the very rigorous discipline of the working-out of the system he clarified much that was dim to his mind: it provided a series of debates with himself on the conflict and relationship between the world of imaginative truth and the real world, but it emerged, not as a set of clear-cut beliefs, but as a set of poetic images through which he has himself apprehended, and through which he can therefore communicate, a particular vision of universal values.

Yeats' 'high breeding' is nowhere seen more luminously than in the quality of his faith. It has no dogma. He belongs, he says, to the very ancient Church where there is an altar but no pulpit.

The old images, the old emotions, awakened again to overwhelming life . . . by the belief and passion of some new soul, are the only masterpieces. The resolution to stand alone, to owe nothing to the past . . . is the result of that individualism of the Renaissance which had done its work when it gave us personal freedom. The soul, which may not obscure or change its form, can yet receive those passions and symbols of antiquity, certain they are too old to be bullies, too well-mannered not to respect the rights of others.*

Myth, legend, tradition, whatever the passions of men have gathered about, are the miracle-makers of the poet. Hence his hatred of realism:

> But actors lacking music
> Do most excite my spleen,
> They say it is more human
> To shuffle, grunt and groan,
> Not knowing what unearthly stuff
> Rounds a mighty scene.†

* *Art and Ideas.*
† *The Old Stone Cross.*

§

Much of Yeats' poetry is difficult, for his symbols are often unfamiliar and have to create and establish their authority within the poems themselves. Eliot's task, for instance, was much easier, because whatever the *reality* of the Christian religion to the modern reader, its *convention*, as it were, is familiar. A knowledge of its tenets, miraculous and ethical, is common property. A poet, even if he cannot presuppose emotional or intellectual acceptance of them, can at least presuppose recognition, a common point from which he can direct his reader's attention towards his own vision. Yeats' poetical abstractions exist, as Shelley's exist, in the mind of man and of nature, but his combinations are strange to us, and both the knowledge of them and the conviction of their spiritual validity have to be generated in his poetry alone.

His great central conception of ultimate reality is the sphere, symbolized in his thought by the moon, while his favorite symbol for human thought and experience is the bobbin. We can approach the conception of complete wholeness in thought only, 'for there's no human life at the full or the dark.' There is only stillness, 'a condition of soul where all is still and finished, all experience wound up upon a bobbin'—that moment of which Eliot speaks in *Burnt Norton:*

At the still point of the turning world. Neither flesh nor fleshless;
Neither from nor towards; at the still point, there the dance is,
But neither arrest nor movement. And do not call it fixity.

Where past and future are gathered. Neither movement
  from nor towards,
Neither descent nor decline. Except for the point, the
  still point,
There would be no dance, and there is only the dance.

That moment is approached but never reached in the
full flower of great civilizations:

Each age unwinds the thread another age has wound,
and it amuses one to remember that before Phidias and his
westward-moving art, Persia fell, and that when full moon
came round again, amid eastward-moving thought, and
brought Byzantine glory, Rome fell; and at the outset
of our westward-moving Renaissance, Byzantium fell:
all things dying each other's life, living each other's
death.*

In human life, the lover drifts near the ultimate revelation:

If I consider deeply, lad and lass
Nerve touching nerve upon that happy ground,
Are bobbins where all time is bound and wound.†

And in *A Woman Young and Old*, there is the same idea:

                          if questioned on
My utmost pleasure with a man
By some new-married bride, I take
That stillness for a theme
Where his heart my heart did seem
And both adrift on the miraculous stream
Where—wrote a learned astrologer—
The Zodiac is changed into a sphere.

Life always whirls the soul away from anything more than
a fleeting breath or glimpse of that transcendence, but

* *A Vision.*
† *The King of the Great Clock Tower.*

man's ceaseless reaching towards the ultimate roundness of the soul's being is his ceaseless struggle to reconcile opposites into unity.

In his two late short plays, *The Full Moon in March* and *The King of the Great Clock Tower*, Yeats gives what to himself was evidently satisfactory concrete expression to this idea. But the poems remain obscure to the general reader, and in *Ego Dominus Tuus* he presents a clearer exposition of his theory of the Mask or anti-self, his idea of what should be man's effort in life and art to approximate the totality of experience. One speaker upbraids the poet:

> *Hic.*   You walk in the moon
> And though you have passed the best of life still trace,
> Enthralled by the unconquerable delusion,
> Magical shapes.
> *Ille.*   By the help of an image
> I call to my own opposite, summon all
> That I have handled least, least looked upon.
> *Hic.* And I would find myself and not an image.

That, says the poet, is the modern heresy. It produces 'the gentle, sensitive mind,' not the creator. Dante, an idle, lecherous man, 'set his chisel to the hardest stone' and created the image of Beatrice. But why not take life as it comes, accept it as it is, and enjoy the good? That, says the poet again, is the solution of the man of action, 'the struggle of the fly in marmalade.' Then, if you are a man of letters, why not study literature instead of meditating directly upon the universe?

> *Ille.* Because I seek an image, not a book.
> Those men that in their writings are most wise
> Own nothing but their blind, stupefied hearts,

but they can call to 'the mysterious one,' the anti-self, and learn from him.

Elsewhere Yeats calls the anti-self a man's 'daemon.' His discipline is to force the man to be consciously dramatic, to wear a mask 'whose lineaments permit the expression of all a man most lacks, and it may be dreads, and of that only.' To apprehend him is, 'among works not impossible, the most difficult'; but the effort nevertheless feeds the hunger in his heart, 'because only the greatest obstacle that can be contemplated without despair, rouses the will to full intensity.'

Hence Yeats' ethic (if one can use the word of something which emerges much more as a general sense of richness, energy and nobility of spirit than as any *scheme* of values) is the ideal of stirring and enkindling living on every side of man's nature: 'the whole man, blood, intellect and imagination running together.' Man contains the universe.

> I mock Plotinus' thought
> And cry in Plato's teeth,
> Death and life were not
> Till man made up the whole,
> Made lock, stock and barrel
> Out of his bitter soul.*

The evils of chance and change are inseparable from the nature of man.

> Everything that man esteems
> Endures a moment or a day.
> Love's pleasure drives his love away,
> The painter's brush consumes his dreams;
> The herald's cry, the soldier's tread

* *The Tower.*

> Exhaust his glory and his might:
> Whatever flames upon the night
> Man's own resinous heart has fed.*

There is no escape, he must wind up his own experience upon the bobbin.

> Endure the toil of growing up;
> The ignominy of boyhood; the distress
> Of boyhood changing into man;
> The unfinished man and his pain
> Brought face to face with his own clumsiness.†

He must endure 'the mirror of malicious eyes,' the consciousness of failure, the sick misery and impotence of unrequited love; all the blank sense of frustration, 'a blind man battering blind men'; 'that old perplexity, an empty purse'; the acceptance of endless disappointment and disillusion:

> Wine shall run thick to the end
> Bread taste sour.

And finally the rage of the heart

> sick with desire
> And fastened to a dying animal.

But the negative implies the positive.

> Love has placed his mansion in
> The place of excrement;
> For nothing can be sole or whole
> That has not been rent.‡

Against fate and fortune, chance and change, stands the glory of man's spirit. That is inviolable, and so is the splendor of his mind, 'intellectual fire' like that of

* *Two Songs from a Play.*
† *Dialogue of the Self and the Soul.*
‡ *Crazy Jane Talks with the Bishop.*

God-appointed Berkeley that proved all things a
    dream,
That this pragmatical, preposterous pig of a world, its
    farrow that so solid seem,
Must vanish on the instant if the mind but change its
    theme.*

And finally there is the unassailable good of the physical
world.

> Curse as you may I sing it through;
> What matter if the knave
> That the most could pleasure you,
> The children that he gave,
> Are somewhere sleeping like a top
> Under a marble flag?
> *I carry the sun in a golden cup,*
> *The moon in a silver bag.*†

Life is none of these things alone; it is the union of them
into a whole. And indeed they are inseparable. The 'con-
secrated blade,' the sword of the spirit, has for its scab-
bard a piece of flowery, silken old embroidery, torn from
some court lady's dress. Material and spiritual are indivisible: Anne Gregory cannot be divided into 'herself' and
her yellow hair, and when the Soul urges the Heart to
'seek out reality, leave things that seem,' to look only on
the fire of Isaiah's coal, for 'salvation walks within,' the
impenitent Heart replies, 'What theme had Homer but
original sin?' The most perfect expression of the idea is
given in *Among School Children*. There, meditating on
age and youth, on life and love, on the bloodlessness of
abstract thought, the heartbreaking sacrifices and denials
of maternity and the religious life, all the empty, incom-

* *Blood and the Moon.*
† *Those Dancing Days Are Gone.*

plete, mocking images which men and women invent and
worship as a substitute for full living, he sums up in two
concrete symbols in the last verse, his conviction of the
indivisibility of body, mind and spirit, of the oneness and
wholeness of man and the universe:

> Labour is blossoming or dancing where
> The body is not bruised to pleasure soul,
> Nor beauty born out of its own despair,
> Nor blear-eyed wisdom out of midnight oil.
> O chestnut tree, great rooted blossomer,
> Are you the leaf, the blossom or the bole?
> O body swayed to music, O brightening glance,
> How can we know the dancer from the dance?

§

> The intellect of man is forced to choose
> Perfection of the life, or of the work.

Yeats chose to be a poet. The poet, he says, 'may not stand
within the sacred house, but lives amid the whirlwinds
that beset its thresholds.' The poet does not work with his
own flesh and blood as material, and does not seek perfection through them, but through paper or parchment:

> Of all the many changing things
> In dreary dancing past us whirled,
> To the cracked tune that Chronos sings,
> Words alone are certain good.

The great poet is, inevitably, a passionate man, but with
him the passions, if they cannot find fulfillment, become
vision, and vision, by rhythm and power, prolongs its
power into poetry. The artist's endless task is to subdue
and subjugate consciousness to form; experience into expression:

Hands, do what you're bid:
Bring the balloon of the mind
That bellies and drags in the wind
Into its narrow shed.

Yeats is the exact opposite of Lawrence as a poet. The great value of Lawrence's philosophy to him was as a hypothetical way of living, which his art might eludicate to himself and to others. His poetry was a gloss on his logos. The value of Yeats' philosophy to him was the antithesis of this: it was to provide a system of thought, a technique of vision, whose discipline ministered to his art by clarifying his thinking into symbols, that is, into material for poetry. His thought busied itself with the subjects common to all thinking human beings: the relation of the actual and the ideal, of body and spirit, of the seen and the unseen, of past and present, of time and the timeless, of the simplicities of the great traditional values and the complexities of living men and women, of good and evil, of life and death, and of the eternal conflict between all these things. But he sought always to give *imaginative* life to all these experiences, to find images and words which should reveal them in a series of unified relationships, of formal and verbal patterns. For he knew that the imagination has some way of lighting on the truth that the reason has not; that it fills our thoughts with the essences of things and not the mere things; that it escapes thus from the barrenness and shallowness of the logical mind into the abundance and depth of nature, and by working in that world between the conscious and the unconscious being, it turns the pride of the conscious intellect into 'the old abounding, nonchalant reverie.'

The best way in which we can see Yeats' 'excited, passionate, fantastical imagination' at work is to examine some of his poetry in detail. Let us take first his sonnet *Leda and the Swan:*

> A sudden blow: the great wings beating still
> Above the staggering girl, her thighs caressed
> By the dark webs, her nape caught in his bill,
> He holds her helpless breast upon his breast.
>
> How can those terrified vague fingers push
> The feathered glory from her loosening thighs?
> And how can body, laid in that white rush,
> But feel the strange heart beating where it lies?
>
> A shudder in the loins engenders there
> The broken wall, the burning roof and tower
> And Agamemnon dead.
>   Being so caught up,
> So mastered by the brute blood of the air,
> Did she put on his knowledge with his power
> Before the indifferent beak could let her drop?

Now in his essay on 'Magic' Yeats has told us that there are certain doctrines on which he bases his vision of universal values and historical myth. These are:

1. That the borders of our minds are ever shifting, and that many minds can flow into one another and create or reveal a single mind, a single energy.
2. That the borders of our memories are as shifting, and are part of one great memory—the memory of Nature herself.
3. That this great mind and memory can be evoked by symbols.

We have already spoken of his belief that it is by the union of opposites that things achieve their greatest power; and there is yet another doctrine of Yeats implied in the last poem, 'that no two civilizations prove or assume the same things, but behind both hides the unchanging experience of simple men and women.'

None of these things is *stated* in the poem, but they are all there in the form of image and implication. Yeats uses the myth of the coming of Zeus to Leda in the form of a swan (from which union Helen of Troy was born), to embody in rhythm and pattern a symbolic integration of all these doctrines.

The basis of the symbol is the common experience of simple men and women, the sexual union. But besides having the common quality of all sexual union, of being the physical mating of the two opposites in the animal creation, male and female, it is the union of humanity and godhead, and of humanity and nature, and the union of the mind and memory of both into one energy: 'Did she put on his knowledge with his power?' It is the fusion too of concrete and abstract; of beauty and might; of gentleness and majesty—the whole in an atmosphere of terror and strangeness. And we can see how this is all created by Yeats in the quality and rhythms of the words he uses: the *energy* of 'A sudden blow: the great wings beating still/ Above the staggering girl . . . ,' 'that white rush,' 'Being so caught up,/ So mastered by the brute blood of the air . . .'; the magnificent, vigorous modeling and movement of the direct sensual picture; and the emotional coloring suggested by 'those terrified vague fingers' and the fierce pulse of 'the strange heart beating where it lies.'

And from that moment of time when all these things

meet, merge and become one, springs Helen, springs the mingled beauty and horror of that great Greek myth.

§

The theme which recurs more often than any other in Yeats' poetry is that of the eternal conflict between body and spirit, between sense and soul. Unlike Eliot, he cannot accept the Christian doctrine on that subject; Crazy Jane has her answer to the Bishop, and many of Yeats' best lyrics are sturdy, pungent and often coarse affirmations of the invulnerable good of the 'blood,' which would have revolted the puritan Lawrence. But what is perhaps his finest poem is the proud and glowing vision of the triumph of the spirit which he called *Byzantium*:

> The unpurged images of day recede;
> The Emperor's drunken soldiery are abed;
> Night resonance recedes, night-walkers' song
> After great cathedral gong;
> A starlit or a moonlit dome disdains
> All that man is,
> All mere complexities,
> The fury and the mire of human veins.
>
> Before me floats an image, man or shade,
> Shade more than man, more image than a shade;
> For Hades' bobbin bound in mummy-cloth
> May unwind the winding path;
> A mouth that has no moisture and no breath
> Breathless mouths may summon;
> I hail the superhuman;
> I call it death-in-life and life-in-death.
>
> Miracle, bird or golden handiwork,
> More miracle than bird or handiwork,
> Planted on the star-lit golden bough,
> Can like the cocks of Hades crow,

Or, by the moon embittered, scorn aloud
In glory of changeless metal
Common bird or petal
And all complexities of mire and blood.

At midnight on the Emperor's pavement flit
Flames that no faggot feeds, nor steel has lit,
Nor storm disturbs, flames begotten of flame,
Where blood-begotten spirits come
And all complexities of fury leave,
Dying into a dance,
An agony of trance,
An agony of flame that cannot singe a sleeve.

Astraddle on the dolphin's mire and blood,
Spirit after spirit! The smithies break the flood,
The golden smithies of the Emperor!
Marbles of the dancing floor
Break bitter furies of complexity,
Those images that yet
Fresh images beget,
That dolphin-torn, that gong-tormented sea.

In the companion poem, *Sailing to Byzantium*, Yeats
contrasts the aging poet and the 'unaging intellect.'

> An aged man is but a paltry thing,
> A tattered coat upon a stick, unless
> Soul clap its hands and sing, and louder sing
> For every tatter in its mortal dress,
> Nor is there singing school but studying
> Monuments of its own magnificence.

These monuments are the triumphs of the world of the
spirit over the world of the senses, of 'the artifice of
eternity' over 'All that man is . . . the fury and the mire
of human veins.'

As a great composite symbol of these monuments Yeats
chooses Byzantium. 'I think that in early Byzantium,

maybe never before or since in recorded history, religious, aesthetic and practical life were one.' Again this symbol, like that of Leda, combines memories of concrete and abstract, the particular and the universal. It recalls certain tangible, material works of art; it is an historical reality; a supreme cultural epoch, with a religious cult steeped in the ideas of the miraculous and the magical; an attitude of mind; a conception of being; and in all its aspects as integral, enduring and incorruptible as the 'golden handiwork,' the 'glory of changeless metal' which the poet chooses as the image dominating the whole vision.

But the unity of the poem is built up of the liquefaction, the fusing and absorbing into one amalgam, of a group of further subsidiary symbols which extend, enforce, enrich and intensify one another in a most intricate and complex pattern. Nor are any of these symbols fixed and rigid in their office; they are full of a mysterious life by which they play both physical and conceptual parts in the complete design, shifting their suggestions from mental and emotional concerns to functions of sound, texture, tone or color, constantly enlarging the circle of attraction they cover, pulling a wider and wider amplitude of reference into the supple network of the poet's reverie.

The first stanza prepares the reader for a vision. It is night, the time when we are nearest release from subjection to the senses, and the purging fires of the spirit can operate. 'Drunken soldiery' (so familiar to Yeats during the 'trouble'), with its implications of sensuality, stupidity, aggression and cruelty, gives concrete physical outline to much of 'the fury and the mire of human veins.' But for the moment they are asleep. The great gong sounds. The gong is the Time symbol: it marks the transition from the temporal to the eternal aspect of things, but it is not that alone. Physically it carries the mind's eye upward from the material bustle of the streets to the transcendental experience symbolized by the dome; and there is the added concept that the gong is the man-invented accompaniment to religious worship. It combines something of sense and something of spirit, and their conjunction gives an added power to the 'gong-tormented' in the last line of the poem. The dome, especially a moonlit dome, immediately suggests all Yeats' feeling in relation to the sphere and the moon. (He first wrote 'distains' for 'disdains,' seeking evidently for a word which could combine the ideas of purification from the sensual and the repudiation of it.)

In the next stanza the vision begins. It is deliberately indefinite. The poet sees, or himself becomes, something free of the sense-world—more ghost than man; for a shade, 'Hades' bobbin bound in mummy-cloth,' may be able to follow the winding path of the maze of existence. The bobbin symbolizes experience *in time*, as we have seen before (the lovers were 'bobbins where all time is bound and wound'). The thread, now being mummy-cloth, acts as a link between living and dead, so that the unwinding may lead to what he speaks of in *All Souls' Night* as 'mummy-truths,' the great universal mind and memory. Thread is spun off the spindle onto the bobbin, so by unwinding the mummy-cloth the shade sheds the last trappings of the sense-world connecting him with 'all that man is,' and so becomes more image than shade, existing

solely in the world of the spirit, 'a mouth that has no mois-
ture and no breath,' and communing there with his peers.
Rapturously he hails that world. It is *totality* of being,
'death-in-life and life-in-death.'

The word value of this stanza is purposely neutral, abstract and toneless. It reaches into that transcendence
where there is no material life, and images of flesh and
blood, color, sound or tangibility are excluded.

In the first stanza it is religion (the great cathedral
gong and dome) which is the symbol of the triumph of
the spirit; now, in the third stanza, art is invoked as the
miraculous manifestation of this triumph. The immortal
beauty of the goldsmith's craft in the shape of a bird can
awaken and welcome the soul, 'can like the cocks of Hades
crow'; can make it scorn material existence just as the
pure line of the dome against the sky carries it soaring in
disdain above human ugliness and confusion.

In the fourth stanza the theme extends to the city, to
the world of human creatures, and to the conflict of the
individual soul. It refers back to *Sailing to Byzantium:*

> O sages standing in God's holy fire
> As in the gold mosaic of a wall,
> Come from the holy fire, perne in a gyre,
> And be the singing masters of my soul.

Blood-begotten spirits can be purged by entering this
eternal spiritual fire which purifies them, but does not
consume; which has neither beginning nor end; which,
like a great Byzantine mosaic, blends rhythm and stillness,
dance and trance, flame and marble.

The last stanza presents the triumphant dramatic clash
and sweep of the conflict of opposites. In a final vision

of the sensual, symbolized by the dolphin, the flood of blood-begotten spirits, weltering among the spawning images of sense, breaks and is calmed into the immortal permanence and peace of 'the soul's magnificence.'

PART II *The Poetic Process*

CHAPTER 7

The Poet and His Medium

> Art deals with what we see, it must first con-
> tribute full-handed that ingredient; it plucks its
> material . . . in the garden of life. . . . But it has
> no sooner done this than it has to take account of a
> *process*. . . .
> The process, that of the expression, the literal
> squeezing out, of value is another affair—with which
> the happy luck of finding has little to do.
> HENRY JAMES. Preface to *The Ambassadors*

'THERE are two ways of disliking art,' said Oscar
Wilde. 'One is to dislike it, and the other is to
like it rationally.' There are few artists who
would not agree with him, and there is a very good reason
for the particular difficulty of finding the right grounds for
an appreciation of poetry, and for the exclusion of everything but a very limited area of its total territory from
popular criticism. The fact that the medium of poetry is
language, that it is the same medium that we all use for
communication with our fellows on all questions of practical living, makes the adequate criticism and enjoyment
of poetry more complex than the criticism and enjoyment
of any of the other major arts. We are accustomed and
conditioned from our earliest youth to the use of language
as a means towards the conduct of life, and when speech
is used as an aesthetic medium most of us need to make
an inner adjustment which we do not need to make
towards the aesthetic use of color, line or sound. For

poetry does not serve the same end as ordinary speech, and the lover of poetry does not ask it to. When Wilde speaks of liking art rationally, he means judging it in terms of its human utility; he means ignoring, or at best, sinking to a secondary importance, the qualities in the creation of poetry which distinguish it, in essence and in nature, from prose. Matthew Arnold's criticism of Goethe is a typically rational liking of poetry:

I honour both the rhythm and the rhyme, by which poetry first becomes poetry; but what is really deeply and fundamentally effective—what is really educative and inspiring, is what remains of the poet when he is trans-lated into prose.

Against this we might put a remark of R. P. Blackmur:

There is, finally, as much difference between words used about a poem, and the poem, as there is between words used about a painting, and the painting. The gap is abso-lute.

This heresy that, although rhythm and rhyme and the whole field of poetic technique are important, they are *less* important than the subject matter, the prose content, with which one is dealing; the idea that poetry is a kind of thinking aloud about life, instead of a revelation of hidden forms of life, has haunted and hampered criticism since earliest times. Poets and critics all down the ages have al-ways had to meet the challenge that poetry must have a rational *use*, and the obvious reply to that is that poetry can and does educate and inspire human nature on the moral plane. As that is a level on which everyone can un-derstand poetry, whereas real artistic sensibility is a much rarer quality, the natural result is the instinct to assess the value of poetry in terms of what it *says* rather than in terms of what it *does;* to judge it not by the quality of consciousness it calls into being, but by the quality of rational activity it is likely to promote. The critical standpoint is then shifted from the poem as a work of art to the poem as an illustration of the personality of the poet, and that in turn leads to criticism like that of Dean Inge on Donne: 'He was no gentleman, and a very equivocal Christian'; or of Eliot on Shelley: 'He was humorless, pedantic, self-centered, and sometimes almost a blackguard.' Obversely, poets who are ethically blameless are praised *as poets* for that reason, as Wordsworth has pointed out:

Readers of moral and religious inclinations, attaching so much importance to the truths which interest them . . . are prone to overrate the Authors by whom those truths are expressed and enforced. They come prepared to impart so much passion to the Poet's language that they remain unconscious how little, in fact, they receive from it.

They provide what we call a stock response, a response which is not justified by what the poetry has aroused, but springs up in the reader as the echo of what he is accustomed to think.

§

Yet the moral preoccupation of much criticism of the past is perhaps no further removed from the realities of poetry than some of the overemphasis on technical detail which has become the fashion of today. Critics approach poetry as matter for scientific analysis as if they were writers in a laboratory, dissecting the texture of the verse regardless of whether the material dissected is in any need of such treatment, or can possibly gain anything from it. The following examination of a couple of almost ultra-simple lines of Milton is an example:

> Hard by, a Cottage chimney smokes,
> From betwixt two aged Okes.

This is simple language, but as poetry the lines are not negligible. We all know that cottage, but the picture we each make is different from our neighbour's. And it is Milton who makes us make that picture. His outline compels us to fill in the detail. His means—and I doubt whether they can be called simple—are drastic economy of detail and musical suggestion. The heavy beat of the first line has nothing to do with the smoke; it suggests squatness and the quality of being solidly based, in the cottage. Statement and rhythm are doing different jobs of work. The rhythm of the second line rises a little at the end— the oaks are tall—and has something carelessly solid in it—the oaks know their own dignity. . . .

Yet the question of how to read poetry concerns all of us, and a mere superficial and generalized appreciation brings very little satisfaction. We all know the type of critic who prefers to be a mere voluptuary of poetic pleasure: 'The reader desires nothing better than to shut critical eyes for a moment in pure enjoyment,' or declares a writer to be the finest living poet, but concludes with a perfunctory genuflection before the mystery of his art: 'Still, one is baffled in the attempt to seize this prodigiously alert talent.' But an encouraging bedside manner combining flattery and evasion will never diagnose an artist. William Empson, likening critics to dogs, says they are of two sorts, 'those who relieve themselves against the flower of beauty, and those, less continent, who afterwards scratch

it up.' He himself, he says, belongs to the second class. 'Unexplained beauty arouses an irritation in me, a sense that this would be a good place to scratch; the reasons that make a line of verse likely to give pleasure, I believe, are like reasons for anything else; one can reason about them.' *
To enjoy poetry rationally in this way is very different from the kind of liking Wilde attacked. It is an exercise in apprehension and discrimination which calls for everything the reader possesses in the way of good readership. Poetry is the art of patterned language. No amount of prose interpretation or elucidation or appreciation or analysis of its various parts by the reader can be the same thing as the poem, though they may be an essential preliminary to the complete enjoyment of the poem. But the poem is the full and unique expression in language of the impact between a certain piece of experience and the poet's consciousness. What the reader can do, is to make the results of this impact as fully conscious to himself as possible, by opening his own faculties as widely as he can to the inflow of all that the poet has communicated by his use of words. 'Attention of perusal . . . is what I at every point . . . absolutely invoke or take for granted,' says Henry James, and this is what the reader can give. He can *live into* the poetry, can re-create it in himself, can feel its vibrations in his own senses, as completely as his capacities and equipment allow. And to do this he must yield himself and be borrowed by the wind that flows through the poem.

> This poem will be you if you will. So let it.
> I do not want you to stand still to get it.

* *Seven Types of Ambiguity.*

You will have it if you go high-speed; it slides in
Between velocities; you will not need to begin
But to have begun and to be going; to have started
To be not separate but flowing; not to be parted
From the smooth spate; be in action; and be there
Not because you are a fraction, but anywhere
Let all and you be all and in relation . . .
Not as a thrown-in stone fall; separation
Is standstill; that is breakdown; that is the end;
You cannot get it so. . . .*

This is the way to read poetry, in a kind of active do-
cility of approach, an eager patience. But to read it fully
requires also a sense of what the poetic discipline *is*, of
what the poet is doing, and of the various ways in which
the effects of poetry operate. It requires, that is, some
study of the relationship of the artist to his medium, of
the marriage of substance and form, of material and making; of what Henry James calls 'the refinements and ecsta-
sies of method.'

§

The soul of man must quicken to creation . . .
Out of the slimy mud of words, out of the sleet and hail
    of verbal imprecisions,
Approximate thoughts and feelings, words that have taken
    the place of feelings,
There springs the perfect order of speech, and the beauty
    of incantation.†

Life as we live it is 'enjoyed,' not contemplated. We
use a completely different adjustment of faculties when
we act and when we re-create the act afterwards in
thought. Art takes us a step further still in detachment:

* Charles Madge.
† T. S. Eliot. *The Rock.*

it is introspection made concrete in another medium. Poetry is a human perspective revealed through a particular apparatus of speech. The substance of poetry is, as we have seen, this human perspective, the vision of reality determined by the nature and environment of the individual poet, his total consciousness of experience. It all comes back, says Henry James, 'to the kind and degree of the artist's prime sensibility, which is the soil out of which his subject springs,' and the test of this is 'the amount of felt life concerned in producing it.' Whether this becomes available to others at all, and the quality of its communication, depends upon a man's mastery of that technique of conveyance which we call poetry; for the important matter in poetry is not the personality of the poet, but the personality of the poem.

Form and content therefore are ultimately indivisible, for the only means we have of arriving at the substance of poetry, the quantity and quality of the poet's experience, is through the means of communication at his disposal. And this can be developed only by personal discipline. As Keats declared: 'The genius of poetry must work out its own salvation in a man: it cannot be matured by law and precept, but by sensation and watchfulness in itself. That which is creative must create itself.' Poetry creates itself from the resources of language.

It follows that the only real criticism of the *art* of poetry is a discussion of these resources. When we are talking about the substance of poetry it is inevitable that we should emphasize aspects of poetry which are detachable, as it were. We can discuss the kind of experience that is behind the poem, the poet's belief or his absence of belief, the depth and soundness of his intellectual capacities, the influence of his environment and the flavor of his personality. All these things may be part of the functional life of the poem, but its organic life is the way in which words are used to make a living whole of all its parts.

§

True poets, says Marianne Moore, present for our inspection 'imaginary gardens with real toads in them'; they interpret human experience in what Mallarmé calls 'a state of crisis'; the poetic temperament, says Keats, 'lives in gusto, be it foul or fair, high or low, rich or poor, mean or elevated'; 'There is only one way of saying what comes to one in ecstasy,' says Hart Crane, 'one works and works over it to finish and organize it perfectly—but fundamentally that doesn't affect one's *way* of saying it.' This cluster of the sayings of poets upon their own art gives us the clue to the basis of poetry. The material of poetry is the matter of life, the toad, seen and felt in a manner of its own, under a peculiar influence, in an imaginary garden.

Now it is clear that Lawrence was right when he described poetry as 'art for *my* sake.' Poetry is the resolution of a state of tension created in the poet's consciousness by experience; it is the external action in which he finds relief from complex emotions and concepts. G. K. Chesterton once defined the artistic temperament as a disease that affects amateurs:

It is a disease which arises from men not having sufficient power of expression to utter and get rid of the element

of art in their being. It is healthful to every sane man to
utter the art within him; it is essential to every sane man
to get rid of the art within him at all costs. Artists of a
large and wholesome vitality get rid of their art easily, as
they breathe easily or perspire easily. But in artists of less
force, the thing becomes a pressure, and produces a
definite pain, which is called the artistic temperament.
. . . There are many real tragedies of the artistic temperament, tragedies of vanity or violence or fear. But the
great tragedy of the artistic temperament is that it cannot
produce any art.*

'One sheds one's sicknesses in books,' said Lawrence, 're-
peats and presents again one's emotions, to be master of
them.' This is very true. A disordered mind, which may
find it impossible to integrate itself into a satisfactory pattern of living, may yet organize the psychic chaos into
poetry of a high order. Baudelaire is an example. In much
of Lawrence's own poetry, however, although it may
have had an anesthetic effect on the tension of his own
feelings, there is little aesthetic experience for the reader.
For, though the struggle between the poet and the raw
problem of living is apparent, there is no corresponding
struggle between the poet and his medium to objectify
his experience fully in terms of art.

We judge the success of poetry by the degree in which
the artist emerges triumphant from this struggle; that is,
from the conflict between his 'state of crisis,' his 'ecstasy,'
and his medium of expression. The result of it is the poem.
'One works and works over it to finish and organize it
perfectly': that is the description of poetic technique. It
is the resistance of the medium to the poet.

* *Heretics.*

§

Poets, like other folk, vary enormously in their methods of work. Wordsworth sometimes waited two years between receiving the original impulse, the flash upon the inward eye, and the final writing of the poem. Keats wrote incessantly and exuberantly:

I find I cannot exist without poetry—without eternal Poetry—half the day will not do—the whole of it—I began with a little, but habit has made me a Leviathan. I had become all in a tremble from not having written anything of late—the Sonnet overleaf did me some good. I slept the better last night for it—this morning, however, I am nearly as bad again.

Keats lived in a perpetual state of 'gusto'; but when the young Welsh poet Dylan Thomas was sent a questionnaire containing the query 'Do you wait for any impulse to write?' he replied,

The writing of the poem is, to me, the physical and mental task of constructing a formally watertight compartment of words . . . to hold a little of the real causes and forces of the creative brain and body. To me the poetical impulse or inspiration is only the sudden, generally physical coming of energy to the constructional, craftsman ability.

And Hart Crane cried despairingly,

Oh, it is hard! One must be drenched in words, literally soaked in them, to have the right ones form themselves into the proper patterns at the right moment.

Dylan Thomas and Crane emphasize what is the most obvious aspect of the poet's craft, his struggle to give concrete expression to 'the real causes and forces of the creative brain and body.' They speak as if the difficulties of finding language were the poet's greatest obstacle. Shelley believed the same. He said that the most glorious poetry in the world was probably a feeble shadow of the original conceptions of the poet, and he likened the process of composition to the gradual fading and cooling of a glowing coal. Yet this aspect is apt to obstruct another point of view—the fact that the relationship of the poet to his medium is not only a conflict but also a collaboration. The poet is not engaged in a struggle with inert passive material which will owe any life it acquires solely to injections of vitality from the poet. He is dealing with a medium which is already alive in its own right, loaded with the riches of tradition, and with every kind of emotional, intellectual, sensuous and pictorial association. Just as the reader, to win the fullest value from poetry, must not 'stand still to get it,' must not be 'separate but flowing,' so the poet, to get all that his medium can give, must blend his own strength with the inherited strength of words. For the experience in the poet's mind when he sits down to write is only one step towards the composition of the poem, and to limit himself to that is to cut himself off from one whole element of his inspiration. Besides what is already there, in a greater or less degree of clarity, there is another force to be reckoned with. This is an incalculable element: it is the web of memories, alliances, affiliations, images and abstractions kindled in his mind during the actual process of construction. These depend largely, of course, on the range and richness of his own consciousness, but many of them arise actively *from the medium itself* as he works in it.

As soon as we face this distinction, we realize the very

different attitudes which poets adopt towards the instrument by which they communicate their own inner vision. Some shrink from its dangers and temptations, looking upon it somewhat as an enemy who must be outwitted; others fraternize with it as an active partner whose suggestions they are only too happy to welcome and to follow. D. H. Lawrence, one of the first type, wrote in a letter:

The essence of poetry in this age of stark and unlovely actualities is a stark directness, without a shadow of a lie, or a shadow of a deflection anywhere. Everything can go, but this stark, bare, rocky directness of statement, this alone makes poetry today.

Eliot commented on this passage: *

This speaks to me of that at which I have long aimed, in writing poetry; to write poetry which should be essentially poetry, with nothing poetic about it, poetry standing naked in its bare bones, or poetry so transparent that we should not see the poetry, but that which we are meant to see through the poetry, poetry so transparent that in reading it we are intent on what the poem *points at*, and not on the poetry, this seems to me the thing to try for. To get *beyond poetry* as Beethoven in his later works, strove to get *beyond music*.

Eliot added that he thought he had written forty or fifty lines of such poetry, but tantalizingly, he does not tell us which they are. Possibly *Burnt Norton* (published since then) is a clue, and some of the Harry-Agatha poem which runs through *The Family Reunion*. Wilfred Owen is perhaps feeling after the same position when he says of his war poems, 'The poetry is the pity,' which has been

* In an unpublished lecture, quoted in *The Achievement of T. S. Eliot* by F. O. Matthiessen.

echoed by Muriel Rukeyser when she says of the facts of the Spanish war, 'Wherever we think of these, the poem is,' and again, 'The poem is the fact.' Laura Riding, too, believes in this creed, arguing that poems, to be true, must be pared of everything which might seduce either the poet himself or his readers into emotions or states of mind which are not 'poetic'; for 'a poem is an uncovering of truth of so fundamental and general a kind that no other name besides poetry is adequate except truth.' The positions of Eliot and Laura Riding are akin, though not perhaps identical, but neither means the same thing by 'stark' poetry as Lawrence did. Another variation of the same basic attitude is that of William Carlos Williams, whose poems aim at keeping the eye strictly on the object. The most famous of his attempts in this method is *Red Wheelbarrow*, which has been extravagantly praised.

> So much depends
> upon
> a red wheel
> barrow
> glazed with rain
> water
> beside the white
> chickens.

Dr. Williams was working here on the Imagist idea of using no words that do not directly contribute to the presentation of the object. His negative success, as it were, is complete: there is nothing whatever superfluous in the poem. The only question is whether there is enough there to make a poem at all: whether the bare bones live and whether their chirping is poetry.

Now it is clear that all these writers, like their prototype Wordsworth before them, have a supreme reverence for something which they regard as Poetic Truth, and which is not equated in their minds with the quality which Keats called Beauty. They have such a reverence for what the poem is to *point at* that they are afraid of the 'poetry' in which it is to be communicated. They fear that the transparency of the medium will be filmed or crusted with matter which may distort or blur or distract attention from the truth or the facts or the object which it is their aim to make shine through undimmed. They believe with Wordsworth that good writing grows of itself from the reality of the passions and from nothing else. They are afraid that words may lead them astray, seducing them into irresponsibilities and irrelevance.

But the difficulty many people have in appreciating such poems is the old one of the baby and the bath-water. Can poetry dispense with everything except 'truth' and remain poetry? Does it not result in the poet's communicating the 'facts' without communicating that state of crisis they produced in the poet, and which gave the facts significance? Perhaps it is true that the medium is only the apple in which the vitamin of poetic truth is assimilated, but if you isolate the vitamin from the apple, and consume it alone in the form of a pellet, the experience is not at all the same thing as eating an apple. What Dr. Williams is doing in this poem is not merely giving the 'truth': he is limiting the truth to a visual observation, and to nothing else. He does this by deliberately stripping his medium to words of one quality only, thus blocking the extension of the experience in any other direction. Language is deliberately inhibited; it is not allowed to function freely.

That there may be a danger on the other side is undeniable. Wordsworth could hardly bear to think of what *might* happen. 'I forbear to speak of an incongruity which would shock the intelligent reader, should the poet interweave any foreign splendours of his own with that which the passion naturally suggests.' The poets who do this, notably the great Elizabethans (to whom Wordsworth's practice would seem equally incongruous and shocking), delight so wholeheartedly in their medium, drench and soak themselves so thoroughly in words, that every phrase and image they use sets another leaping at its heels by some association of thought or feeling springing from their language. It is these reverberations which the advocates of poetic truth distrust as falsifying the experience. And indeed they may. Hart Crane in *The Bridge* is often drowned as well as drenched. A poet may be either master or slave to his medium, but his business is not to deny any of the resources at his disposal, but to select and control them; to make them beneficent instead of beguiling. And if we read poetry carefully, it is impossible not to note on every page how the collaboration between artist and medium works, in large ways and small. When Eliot, for instance, makes Mr. Prufrock reflect that there will be

> time for a hundred indecisions
> And for a hundred visions and revisions,
> Before the taking of a toast and tea,

we may guess that it was the actual word 'visions' which caused him to follow it with 'revisions'—an inspiration provided *from his medium*, not from the concept of the whole poem in his mind before he began to write. But the play upon the words, and the analogy of sound, with the opposition, or extension, of sense, which the addition brings, definitely enriches the content of the whole mental picture.

Even the necessity of finding a rhyme may prove an asset instead of a liability to the poet. In the fourth verse of *Byzantium*, for example, where Yeats describes the purging but nonconsuming fire through which the blood-begotten spirits pass, as 'An agony of flame that cannot singe a sleeve,' we can imagine him faced with the necessity of expressing the idea of a fire which does not devour, and at the same time of providing a rhyme for 'leave.' From that technical necessity may have come in a flash the vision of a Byzantine mosaic with a figure whose flowing robes hang unsinged over a tongue of bright flame, and a line which combines triumphantly an abstract concept with a vivid pictorial image; an image, too, which strengthens the particular atmosphere of the whole poem.

§

Poets know that their main function is to be master of a discipline, for only so can the moment of ecstasy, the state of crisis, be made fully available as poetic substance. The mastery of his technique gives the poet a surer and subtler interpretation of his consciousness, just as the training of a dancer or an athlete gives him a surer and suppler control over the muscles of his body. As Blake says: 'Without unceasing Practise nothing can be done.

Practise is Art. If you leave off you are Lost.' Or as Emily
Dickinson put it, with a wider significance:

> Essential oils are wrung;
> The attar from the rose
> Is not expressed by suns alone,
> It is the gift of screws.

It is quite possible, of course, that the poet's technical
achievements may be sure but slight. Many minor poets
achieve a reputation in their own day above their real
merit because of their firm hold on a pleasing technique
quite adequate to any content they may have to express.
Their voices may be of small compass, but they have been
well trained. Elinor Wylie was a poet of this caliber. And
a writer with a quality of imaginative vision far beyond
such poets may be less available to the reader because of
an incapacity to project and control it in language. Hence
the fitful and spasmodic quality we find in Hart Crane, or
in D. H. Lawrence, or in Richard Eberhart, where passages of great force and beauty alternate with slabs of
slack and inactive matter which the poet, through in-
competence or carelessness, has not fully energized into
living tissue.

Poets such as Dylan Thomas, and many of the Surrealists, appear to make of much of their writing simply a technical discipline. They do not care whether the content of
certain poems is anything beyond merely private notation
of psychic experience. Such poets are at the opposite extreme from Wordsworth and Williams, literalists of the
subconscious instead of literalists of the fact. In the one
we miss the imaginary garden around the real toad, in the
other we miss the toad which should be a focus for our

apprehension of the imaginary garden. With both the average reader is dissatisfied, but the poet himself believes that he has found the true pattern of words for the truth of his unique and individual vision.

And that is his sole problem. It must all be fumbled gently and patiently out, as Henry James said of the idea for a novel; or as Herbert Read expresses it in our contemporary critical jargon,

In the process of poetic composition words rise into the conscious mind as isolated objective 'things' with a definite equivalence in the poet's state of mental intensity. They are arranged or composed in a sequence or rhythm which is sustained until the mental state of tension in the poet is exhausted or released by this objective equivalence.

§

This 'objective equivalence' is the poem, and the 'fumbling' by which the artist gets it out of himself is very largely a matter of hard work, of pure critical intelligence. We have only to go to the poets themselves (always the best authorities on poetry) to see that this is so. Coleridge says genius needs *talent* properly to manifest itself. Eliot declares that 'probably the larger part of the labour of an author in composing his work is critical labour; the labour of sifting, combing, constructing, expunging, correcting, testing.' He speaks elsewhere of a certain 'tough reasonableness' in lyric poetry, just as Matthew Arnold emphasizes its 'fundamental brainwork.' Yeats, describing his own method of composing, says that nothing at all of the final form was set down on the first day of work upon a poem. The second day he might get out the rhyme scheme for the first stanza; and so it went on. Keats, again, describes 'the innumerable compositions and decompositions which take place between the intellect and its thousand materials before it arrives at that trembling, delicate and snail horn perception of beauty.'

Technique, in fact, is the purposive application of ingenuity.

CHAPTER 8

Visions and Revisions

Poetic experiences are not isolated, and without
reference to anything else in the poet's spiritual
make-up. On the contrary, they may be synthetic,
quintessential expressions of his whole nature and
experience.

J. W. N. SULLIVAN. *Beethoven*

THE first question to determine about any poem is
the 'mode of consciousness' in which the poet
conceived it. 'There is only one way of saying
what comes to one in ecstasy,' Hart Crane declares, and
the success of the whole poem will depend upon the poet's
finding that way.

We say the 'success' of the poem, not its value. The
value of a poem cannot be assessed apart from the *quality*
of its substance. Wordsworth said poetry was the spontaneous overflow of powerful feelings, but he modified the
statement by continuing:

Poems to which any value can be attached were never
produced on any variety of subjects but by a man who,
being possessed of more than usual organic sensibility,
had also thought long and deeply.

Keats, whom we think of as the great poet of the emotions and the senses, aimed at a far more comprehensive
'substance,' and spoke of 'the yearning passion I have for
the beautiful, connected and made one with the ambition
of my intellect.' 'Every thought I think is thought, and

every line I write is writing,' said Newman, and it is as good a motto for verse as for prose. While we have all to be on our guard against automatically equating the intellectual and emotional truth of an author with his poetic ability, we do well to remind ourselves that no poem in which the 'substance' is trivial, superficial, trite, feeble or false, can have 'value' as poetry.

All poetry can be said to be either narrative or dramatic in spirit. The poet is telling a story, or describing a scene or a person, or else he is an actor in a psychological situation. In any case, his treatment of his theme or subject will depend entirely upon the psychological coloring he sees it through or the psychological angle or plane he sees it from. We find Keats writing,

> O Poesy! for thee I hold my pen,
> That am not yet a glorious denizen
> Of thy wide heaven—should I rather kneel
> Upon some mountain-top until I feel
> A glowing splendour round about me hung,
> And echo back the voice of thine own tongue?
> O Poesy! . . .

Here we have one mood in which a poet may look at his art. If we turn to Marianne Moore's *Poetry*, though the subject is the same, the attitude has totally changed:

> I, too, dislike it: there are things that are important be-
>   yond all
>   this fiddle.
> Reading it, however, with a perfect contempt for it,
>   one discovers in
> it after all, a place for the genuine.

As Marianne Moore says in another poem, 'Ecstasy affords the occasion and expediency determines the form';

so that in any formal examination of a poem, the first aim is to catch the quality of 'ecstasy' which has occasioned it, and then to examine the quality of the 'expediency' which has formed its outline. Let us take two complete poems on the same subject.

For a Lamb

I saw on the slant hill a putrid lamb,
Propped with daisies. The sleep looked deep,
The face nudged in the green pillow
But the guts were out for crows to eat.

Where's the lamb? whose tender plaint
Said all for the mute breezes.
Say, he's in the wind somewhere,
Say, there's a lamb in the daisies.

RICHARD EBERHART

Death Bereaves Our Common Mother Nature Grieves for My Dead Brother

Lamb dead, dead lamb,
He was, I am,
Separation by a tense
Baulks my eyes' indifference.
Can I see the lately dead
And not bend a sympathetic head?
Can I see lamb dead as mutton
And not care a solitary button?

STEVIE SMITH

Here we have exactly the same situation dramatized in two different tones. In the first there is a concrete physical picture, the slant hill, the decaying body, the daisies, the face nudged in the green pillow; and there is a complexity of emotions and ideas: beauty and disgust, the horror of mortality, the extinction of youth and innocence, the interrelationship of animate and inanimate nature, and the universal mystery of life and death. But the dominating mood is one of gentleness. The image of the putrid body with the guts out is tempered by the vision of infant sleep, the daisies and the lamb's living bleat matching the soft breezes. The simplicity and movement of the verse and of the vocabulary all emphasize the pity and questioning such a sight brings.

In the second poem, such a response is impossible. It is sharply inhibited by the tone of light but precise irony. The temptation to regard the death of the lamb as closely linked with human mortality is stated—can one really remain indifferent in the face of the death of any living creature?—and is then rapidly transformed by the satiric reminder that the same situation really arises every time dead lamb appears on the dinner table. And here again, the shift in tone is established by the movement and language of the poem, which combines both banter and seriousness until the last couplet sets its seal upon the ironic intent.

§

But these are illustrations of simple differences of tone or mood, and the differences in the quality of 'ecstasy' go much deeper than that. The kind of apprehension of experience from which the poem springs may be simply a widening or a sharpening of what we might call the normal way of apprehending experience, or it may be some altogether abnormal approach which is peculiar to the poet. For instance, the theme of Keats' *Ode on a Grecian Urn* and that of Yeats' *Byzantium* are much the same—the imperishable vitality of art in comparison with the mortality of the life of the senses. Keats approaches that theme directly, in the form of an explicit reverie, on a particular Greek pot. Yeats transmutes his material into a symbolic and complex vision, and removes us to a strange and unfamiliar plane of experience which is created entirely by his poetic method. And we must reach that plane before we can live fully into the poem. So that unless the character of the poet's creative impulse, his 'state of crisis,' is rightly seized by the reader, the whole reading of the poem will inevitably be faulty. When Harriet Monroe proposed to cut Lawrence's *Ballad of Another Ophelia*, he wrote protesting that it was impossible, and that she could not have suggested it if she had entered imaginatively into its world. 'This poem has got the quality of a troublesome dream that seems incoherent but is selected by another sort of consciousness.'

At no other period, perhaps, has there been so wide a gamut of poetic modes as during the last twenty years. The weakening of tradition, the lack of communal purpose and the resulting emphasis on individualism all throw the poet back on those aspects of his art which differentiate him from his fellows, and from the prose approaches to experience. In the postwar period there was a deliberate cultivation, amounting very often to a deliberate forcing, of individual traits and oddities of vision. In poetry of the past the step from life or thought to poetry was usually much more direct and simple. The poet colored his material with his own personality, he selected it according to his own tastes, but he did not dissociate his poetic personality entirely from his workaday personality. He did not isolate poetry from ordinary living as jealousy as has been the modern fashion. Robert Frost has written good poetry in the old tradition, but he is an exception, and the straightforward lyric of simple direct intensity of thought and feeling is very rare. Richard Eberhart writes in that mode sometimes, and Robert Graves. But far more often the poet does not simply bring passion to bear upon a situation seen by all of us in the same general terms. He substitutes for those general terms some special terms of his own which metamorphose the situation. In the first verse of *Rhapsody on a Windy Night* Eliot describes how at night the whole organization of ordinary living seems broken up: the different lighting produces a different pattern, a 'lunar synthesis' which for the time being blots out the familiar outlines:

> Whispering lunar incantations
> Dissolve the floors of memory
> And all its clear relations,
> Its divisions and precisions. . . .

The modes of consciousness in which poetry is written operate in much the same way. At the extreme of removal from the normal we have a poet like Rimbaud, who regarded the poet's vision as something so completely antipathetic to the common man's that he must deliberately break down everything which controls the conscious human personality. Only out of the resulting chaos could the new creative vision of the poet's world be formed. Hence drugs and alcohol or anything which disturbs the balance of the reason, and frees the forces and faculties from its shackles, seemed to him valuable as aiding the new creative synthesis. Poe's work was largely produced in the same way, and perhaps a good deal of Hart Crane's was written under the influence of the same idea. But this is the extreme statement of a process which we can see at work, consciously and unconsciously, in a great deal of contemporary poetry. The material of the poem is, as it were, swallowed, and then digested and assimilated into a new body by the individual metabolism of the poet. Marianne Moore may transfigure a human situation by placing it in an imaginary zoo; or Ransom transform its proportions by the use of a grotesque irony; or Wallace Stevens heighten the pitch with the clavier, or the color with tropical vegetation; or Edith Sitwell transport the modern world into the queer pantomime world of *Clowns' Houses;* or Cummings may enforce a new angle of discernment by a new arrangement of speech and punctuation; or Yeats may transpose the problem of good and evil into a duet for Crazy Jane and the Bishop. Or the whole thing may be presented in the form of a symbol, as Hart Crane attempted to do in *The Bridge,* or its reality may be built up by suggestion and accretion from a multitude of sources, as in Eliot, or its significance emphasized by showing it in terms of another age or civilization, as in Pound.

§

It is this variety of poetic sensibilities in contemporary poetry which accounts for the wide range in experimental technique. The poet who introduces significant technical changes will always be found to have been driven into doing so by psychological needs, by the pressure of his 'state of crisis.' 'A style, a rhythm, to be significant, must also embody a significant mind, must be produced by the necessity of a new form for a new content,' says Eliot. And just as our age has produced a wide divergence of modes of apprehension, so it has produced a wide divergence of techniques of communication, of unmistakable personal idioms. Apart from those we have mentioned above, we might list Sandburg, Vachel Lindsay, Robinson Jeffers, Laura Riding, and among the younger writers Eberhart, Horace Gregory, Auden, Spender, Dylan Thomas and F. T. Prince, each of whom, in addition to the common tones and rhythms which mark them as 'early twentieth century,' has a distinctive 'voice' to communicate a distinctive quality of imaginative living. 'Every age has its false alarms,' as Hopkins says, and a personal idiom need not imply very much. None of the older minor poets, except perhaps Stevens, has shown any development or further maturing since their early achievement, and their peculiar traits have in some cases hardened into tricks, and their art into artificiality. But nevertheless each of these poets demands of the reader an active response to a specialized vision, each creates a reality by handling words in some sharply contemporary or personal way, each expands the traditional or conventional approach to experience by producing a resistance which the reader is forced to meet. A poet who does *not* ask any such effort of the reader, and can yet give the impression of modernity, is, of course, always much more popular with the public at large than any experimental writer, since most readers are naturally lazy, and few are really interested in art. The popularity of Edna St. Vincent Millay is an example. She possesses most richly that gusto in which the poetic temper exists, and her sensibility is a twentieth century sensibility, even if one does not feel it to belong to the nineteen thirties. But the pressure of the personal consciousness of either her environment or her experience has never been sufficiently strong for her to be driven to forge a new technique in which to express it. She expresses a twentieth century romantic temperament in a nineteenth century romantic vehicle. Her psychological needs are amply satisfied in words and rhythms which have carried emotion many times before, and therefore awaken an immediate response in the romantic reader. The same might be said of Elinor Wylie and Sara Teasdale, for all their extremely sensitive craftsmanship.

§

The 'inspiration'—the mood or mode in which the experience has been conceived—is only the first step in poetic creation: it is the 'occasion.' Now the poet's real task begins. The poem has got to become self-supporting, the poet has to find the 'expedient' which shall set his consciousness in flight. D. H. Lawrence wrote of a friend's poems: 'I can see all the poetry at the *back* of your verses —but there isn't much inside the lines. It's the rhythm and the sound that don't penetrate the blood.' Poetry is essentially *movement*. Its form is a rhythm. It is a 'body swayed to music.' But this rhythm is not a matter of external sound pattern only, it is a fusion of two elements, abstract and concrete, which it is the poet's aim to identify.

The most difficult and elusive term in any discussion of poetry is, perhaps, the word 'imagination.' It is used in the loosest and vaguest way as a convenient term to cover any aspect of the poet's matter or manner, and a serious analysis of it, as in Coleridge's *Biographia Literaria*, is apt to be too abstract and metaphysical for the average reader. But some attempt to give it a meaning must be made. Let us take Coleridge's description of it as 'the power of reducing multitude into unity of effect, and modifying a series of thoughts by some one predominating thought or feeling.' The 'one predominating thought or feeling' immediately suggests that it is closely associated with the sense of crisis or ecstasy from which all poetry springs. In fact, this condition is frequently called 'imaginative vision.' Coleridge elsewhere calls the imagination the 'shaping power,' which links up with 'the power of reducing multitude into unity of effect.' So that it is the fusion of these two things—the faculty of perceiving experience in a special way, and the shaping of the complexities of that perception into its perfect proportions. The mere discipline of arranging material with intelligence and feeling into a sound pattern will not make poetry. Roy Campbell wrote somewhat rudely of poets who achieve that only:

> You praise the self-restraint with which they write—
> I'm with you there, of course;
> They use the snaffle and the curb all right
> But where's the bloody horse?

Unless the material has been perceived with the imaginative vision, the form will be mechanic instead of organic;

it will be fixed and dead, instead of having a flow, a movement like that of a living body, never in any rigid state of exact adjustment, held together by a vital cohesion which controls blood, nerves and articulation into perfection of free functioning.

To this end, therefore, the poet bends all the technical discipline of which he is master: to establish a unity in terms of his total intention, to relate parts duly to the whole. Given the moment of imaginative vision, the tone will be set for the whole poem. That will be the center of balance for the whole composition, holding it in equipoise, and giving it its central meaning. This may not be openly *stated* in the poem at all, and it may not be a *subject* in the sense that Lucy Gray is the subject of the poem of that name, but it will be an attitude, a theme, a mood or a perception round which the whole poem accretes.

In some poems, indeed in the majority of poems of past ages, this psychological unity is accompanied by a unity of logical intellectual structure which is at once apparent to the reader. But today, the revulsion from the often too facile and superficial technique of the Victorians and Georgians, and the profound influence of the French Symbolists through the channel of Eliot and Pound, have set a fashion for the oblique approach, for the method where the thought pattern becomes implicit instead of explicit. Some examples of each method will make the matter clearer.

A poem where the attitude of mind is not openly stated, but where the controlling force is strictly logical, is Empson's *Legal Fiction:*

Law makes long spokes of the short stakes of men.
Your well fenced out real estate of mind
No high flat of the nomad citizen
Looks over, or train leaves behind.

Your rights extend under and above your claim
Without bound; you own land in Heaven and Hell;
Your part of earth's surface and mass the same,
Of all cosmos' volume, and all stars as well.

Your rights reach down where all owners meet, in Hell's
Pointed exclusive conclave, at earth's centre
(Your spun farm's root still on that axis dwells);
And up, through galaxies, a growing sector.

You are nomad yet; the lighthouse beam you own
Flashes, like Lucifer, through the firmament.
Earth's axis varies; your dark central cone
Wavers, a candle's shadow, at the end.

The content of this poem is communicated in two dominating images, one drawn from legal, the other from mathematical terminology. The key is in the title. A legal fiction is an imaginary extension of human rights which has no basis in actual fact. The dictionary defines it as 'a rule of law which assumes as true, and will not allow to be disproved, something which is false but not impossible.' The particular instance of this on which the poem is founded is the statement *Cujus et solum, ejus est usque ad coelum et ad inferos:* 'He to whom the soil belongs, owns all above it up to the sky, and all the depths below it.' The poet transfers this 'fiction' to man's ownership of his mind, and the irony which is the 'mood' of the poem and which is implicit in the fiction is stated in the image of the first line:

Law makes long spokes of the short stakes of men.

Man's ownership of land, whatever grandiose claims the law makes for him, depends, in fact, upon the limitations of his human conditions. There is an analogue to this in the realm of the mind. Man may claim that his ownership is absolute; that he can cut himself off from cramping human limitations; that he can escape from that circumscribed plot where he is confined by relationships with his fellow creatures; that he can dwell in heaven or hell, the earth's center or the stars; that his mind is his own, and that it is free, unshackled, piercing, proud. But in fact, what do these high claims amount to? The claims of the mind in the regions of heaven and hell are unrealistic. They are based upon a fiction. Man's vision is actually a mere flash in the firmament, failing as Lucifer failed and fell. Forces beyond the control of man, exemplified here by the variations in the earth's axis, limit his powers and reduce the proud, flashing beam to darkness and the wavering slightness of a candle's shadow.

In addition to the legal image, the content of the poem is further illustrated by a strict geometrical figure built upon the circle, the axis, the sector and the cone, which the curious reader can trace for himself. The interrelationship of the two main figures is a fine piece of intellectual ingenuity, worked out with the acumen we associate with the law and the precise lucidity we associate with a mathematical diagram. It is questionable, however, whether the concern of the reader with the visual and intellectual framework, and indeed the demands which the poet makes on the reader's factual knowledge of these, does not somewhat cramp his imaginative apprehension of the poem as a whole, and ob-

struct his spontaneous appreciation of the thought by
the attention he is forced to pay to the intrinsic machinery.

At the opposite extreme from Empson's strict, even
constricted, control of his substance, we might place
Edna St. Vincent Millay's treatment of an abstract theme
in her sonnet *Euclid Alone Has Looked on Beauty Bare:*

> Euclid alone has looked on Beauty bare.
> Let all who prate of Beauty hold their peace,
> And lay them prone upon the earth and cease
> To ponder on themselves, the while they stare
> At nothing, intricately drawn nowhere
> In shapes of shifting lineage; let geese
> Gabble and hiss, but heroes seek release
> From dusty bondage into luminous air.
>
> O blinding hour, O holy, terrible day,
> When first the shaft into his vision shone
> Of light anatomized! Euclid alone
> Has looked on Beauty bare. Fortunate they
> Who, once only and then far away,
> Have heard her massive sandal set on stone.

Here the poet's condition of heightened sensibility arises
from the realization of that moment of pure intellectual
beauty

> When first the shaft into his vision shone
> Of light anatomized!

The tone should be that of a sudden emotional apprehension of the awe and loveliness of pure naked abstractions; but neither the substance nor the shaping of the
poem creates any feeling of emotional or intellectual *intensity* at all. There is a general emotional excitement, but
it is not focused to a point. The author attempts to

supply it by a pseudo-poetic vocabulary—'prate,' 'lay them prone,' 'the while'—which is intended to remove us from the atmosphere of everyday into the realm of Beauty; and by a group of high-sounding phrases and images which are, however, loose and general, and in no living relationship with her central moment. They will not bear analysis; they create no sweep or flow in the mind; they are empty, splashy, exclamatory. The responses of the poet to the idea of Beauty are stock responses, immediately evoking the reaction of facile epithets like 'blinding,' 'holy,' 'terrible' (compare Yeats' precise use in 'a terrible beauty is born' in *Easter 1916*). Nor is there anything of significance generated in the mind by the opposition of geese and heroes, nor in the symbolizing of the intellectual beauty of 'light anatomized' as the *sound* of a massive sandal set on stone. The rhythm and language thus become inactive and irresponsible; they lose all precision of outline, straining for sublimity, and falling upwards into vacuity: the light becomes a blur, the anatomy shifting shapes of nothing.

§

We may say of these two poems that the tension in one is almost too tight, in the other much too loose; the poise of one is a little cramped, the other sprawls. As an example, therefore, of something which holds a more perfect balance between intellect and emotion, and between abstract and concrete, let us take John Crowe Ransom's fine poem *The Equilibrists:*

Full of her long white arms and milky skin
He had a thousand times remembered sin.

Alone in the press of people traveled he,
Minding her jacynth and myrrh and ivory.

Mouth he remembered: the quaint orifice
From which came heat that flamed upon the kiss,
Till cold words came down spiral from the head,
Gray doves from the officious tower illsped.

Body: it was a white field ready for love.
On her body's field, with the gaunt tower above,
The lilies grew, beseeching him to take,
If he would pluck and wear them, bruise and break.

Eyes talking: Never mind the cruel words,
Embrace my flowers but not embrace the swords.
But what they said, the doves came straightway flying
And unsaid: Honor, honor, they came crying.

Importunate her doves. Too pure, too wise,
Clambering on his shoulder, saying, Arise,
Leave me now, and never let us meet,
Eternal distance now command thy feet.

Predicament indeed, which thus discovers
Honor among thieves, Honor between lovers.
O such a little word is Honor, they feel!
But the gray word is between them cold as steel.

At length I saw these lovers fully were come
Into their torture of equilibrium:
Dreadfully had forsworn each other, and yet
They were bound each to each, and did not forget.

And rigid as two painful stars, and twirled
About the clustered night their prison world,
They burned with fierce love always to come near,
But Honor beat them back and kept them clear.

Ah, the strict lovers, they are ruined now!
I cried in anger. But with puddled brow

Devising for those gibbeted and brave
Came I descanting: Man, what would you have?

For spin your period out, and draw your breath,
A kinder saeculum begins with death.
Would you ascend to Heaven and bodiless dwell?
Or take your bodies honorless to Hell?

In Heaven you have heard no marriage is,
No white flesh tinder to your lecheries,
Your male and female tissue sweetly shaped
Sublimed away, and furious blood escaped.

Great lovers lie in Hell, the stubborn ones
Infatuate of the flesh upon the bones;
Stuprate, they rend each other when they kiss;
The pieces kiss again—no end to this.

But still I watched them spinning, orbited nice.
Their flames were not more radiant than their ice.
I dug in the quiet earth and wrought the tomb
And made these lines to memorize their doom:—

Equilibrists lie here; stranger, tread light;
Close, but untouching in each other's sight;
Mouldered the lips and ashy the tall skull,
Let them lie perilous and beautiful.

The thesis is the age-long conflict between love and honor, between material and spiritual values. The poet states the argument in the form of a parable of two lovers. Their love symbolizes, and is symbolized by, all the joys of the bodily senses: 'male and female tissue sweetly shaped'; the white flesh which is tinder to lechery; the gleam of jacynth, the perfume of myrrh, the texture of ivory, the warmth of the flame of physical union, the fertility of field, the blossoming and sweetness of lilies.

The symbols of the spirit are the gaunt tower of the head, gray doves and the little gray word Honor, cold as steel. And so they remain, in this torture of equilibrium, two stars bound each in its rigid course, 'orbited nice,' each in its separate prison. (In Empson's poem the mind also swings to the spinning of the universe, but Ransom's image of the stars is more explicitly humanized; it has both intellectual and emotional force, and in addition, the suggestion of physical attraction and repulsion.) The poet, puzzled, balances the issue. Is it better to be without a body in heaven, or without honor in hell; to achieve light without heat, or heat without light? True, honor is a deathless value, but think of an existence where physical love is 'sublimed away'; even if life after death is kinder, heaven cannot give them what they have lost upon earth. But again, an eternity of nothing but physical love must be hell itself . . .

The psychological coloring which creates the peculiar atmosphere of this poem is the irony with which the poet presents the predicament. There is no solution; all we *know* is that the grave brings dissolution in both lips and skull, to both flesh and brain. The whole principle of the poem is that of balance: one set of ideas, one set of images, hangs in the scale against the other. And this principle communicates itself to the verse, which holds a level, poised rhythm throughout, without any fall or rise in pitch, any loosening or tightening of tension, with the rhymes in the symmetrical four-lined stanza chiming in pairs, and an exactness and sustained decorum in the vocabulary.

§

We have so far considered poems where the 'meaning'
is made definite and immediately intelligible to the reader
by the method of presentation: it is explicit. But now we
will examine the method by which the poet establishes
the psychological unity without the prop of a clear logical structure: it is implicit. Take, for instance, Yeats' *Leda
and the Swan*, where the moment of ecstasy which is the
'occasion' is the perception of the act of copulation embodied in that myth as a center, bringing to a focus the
three ideas of the conflict and union of opposites, the
partaking in a common universal memory, and the en-
gendering of a new culture. The whole poem is constructed round that. Every phrase, every picture, every
line of movement, is directed towards that. It controls the
symmetry of the whole composition, but there is no *statement* of it as the theme: it only emerges from the totality
of the poem. Or take an example where the method and
tone, the use of rhythm and language, are quite unlike
anything we have yet quoted—the second poem in those
called *Voyages* by Hart Crane:

> And yet this great wink of eternity,
> Of rimless floods, unfettered leewardings,
> Samite sheeted and processioned where
> Her undinal vast belly moonwards bends,
> Laughing the wrapt inflections of our love;
>
> Take this Sea, whose diapason knells
> On scrolls of silver snowy sentences,
> The sceptred terror of whose sessions rends
> As her demeanors motion well or ill,
> All but the pieties of lovers' hands.

And onward, as bells off San Salvador
Salute the crocus lustres of the stars,
In these poinsettia meadows of her tides,—
Adagios of islands, O my Prodigal,
Complete the dark confessions her veins spell.

Mark how her turning shoulders wind the hours,
And hasten while her penniless rich palms
Pass superscription of bent foam and wave,—
Hasten, while they are true,—sleep, death, desire,
Close round one instant in one floating flower.

Bind us in time, O Seasons clear, and awe.
O minstrel galleons of Carib fire,
Bequeath us to no earthly shore until
Is answered in the vortex of our grave
The seal's wide spindrift gaze toward paradise.

The theme of the poem is the desire that the union of human lovers should be fulfilled by a mystical union with the sea—a symbol here of the eternal unity and the supreme beloved.

The strange syntax of the opening 'And yet . . .' establishes obliquely the idea of the eternal continuity of the sea's being, and of its infinite expanse and freedom. But the 'wink' contracts the conception to a particular moment in time and space, combined with a visual image of the sea gleaming in the moonlight, and a hint of the laughter referred to in the last line of the verse. In the fourth line the sexual image carries the mind from the concept of the sea to the instance of the human lovers, but the last line underscores the distinction between them: the attitude of the sea is that of a kindly superiority to 'the wrapt inflections of our love' ('wrapt' carries the double significance of 'embrace' and 'rapture,' and 'inflections' that of 'speech' and 'enfolding').

In the second stanza, one lover addresses the other: Consider this sea . . . whose compass of tones is written in wave-crests breaking into foam on silvery sands. But those tones are 'knelled' as well as 'spelled' because these written records are *sentences* in the double sense of written characters and of judgments passed by a supreme judge, which rend (pass sentence of parting) with a greater or lesser degree of severity, on everything except the devotion of lovers. The whole stanza is a crowded and interrelated imagery of the ideas of the death-sentence, the tolling bell, the written judgment, and the absolute monarchy of the supreme being over everything except human love.

The next stanza pursues the idea, and at the same time introduces a purely visual image of the sea's beauty. And further on the bell buoys greet the reflection of the stars, strewn in the water like crocuses growing in a meadow. But the meadows here are the poinsettia-colored fiery sea around the Caribbean islands. The tolling of the buoys in the calm sea is slow and lingering (an adagio), and to this tempo the islands are assimilated, for spaced out on the sea's surface they repeat for the eye the adagio music of the bells, while the movement of the boat among them completes the quiet rhythm. These islands are fragments broken from the mainland and lie on the sea's surface (veined with foam) as a confession of the merciless judgments of severance referred to in the previous stanza. The address 'O my Prodigal' is obscure, but it appears more likely that it refers to the sea than to the lover, of whom we know nothing. The idea of prodigality is hinted at again in the 'penniless rich palms' of the next stanza, and perhaps it refers back to the golden stars strewn so lavishly in the water.

But the address to the lover continues in the fourth stanza: See how the tides change with the hours ('her turning shoulders' suggests again a parallel with the 'inflections' of the lovers) and hasten while the sea writes with the superscription of foam and wave a promise of fulfillment for the lovers. Seize the instant while everything is propitious, when sleep, death, desire can be unified in one supreme moment of blossoming.

The opening line of the final stanza invokes the transcendent instant—the auspicious moment, the 'seasons clear,' for mariners setting out on a voyage, asking that the lovers may be united in that hour in a spirit of mystic communion. Then the waves of the Caribbean, musical and phosphorescent, are addressed with the entreaty that the bodies of the lovers be not cast upon the shore, until the spiritual union between them and the eternal being is consummated—some such union as is typified in the yearning gaze of the seal, looking out over the face of the waters towards the home of the spirit.

In this poem, there is no statement of the theme at all. Its thought form is in the interweaving of a group of ideas active in a moment of intense emotional experience —the mystic revelation of the union of all individual life in a larger life. As in the Leda sonnet, the symbol of the union is sexual love, but the emphasis here is not upon the symbol, but upon the thing symbolized (there is but one sexual image in the poem, and it is not developed)— the security and assurance of that future union to which the death wish is here the prelude. Against this is suggested the idea of the separateness of all human creatures not united by love, and the implacability and uncertainty of their fate apart from this instinct of communion with some infinite power.

The interrelated elements of this vision—the infinity and eternity of the sea, the knell of death, the sentence of the human soul to be divided against itself and from its fellows in life—are spelled and knelled out in a most complex interweaving of images and language, in which suggestions glance off one another, color one another, sustain, sharpen or soften one another in almost every line. Since there is no explicit logical content in the poem, the words and images have to bear the whole weight of revealing the theme, the tone, the emotional coloring, by their power of direct or indirect suggestion and reverberation, by their richness and fertility of significance and scope. This inevitably means that the poem is difficult. It can communicate much without an understanding of its thought, for it moves with a beautiful grace in its inflections, sustaining a rhythm of the rise and fall and swell of 'bent foam and wave,' lighted by an iridescence of emotional and pictorial coloring. But it takes many readings to arrive at any sort of clarity of exposition, and to a realization of how loaded, packed and concentrated is the use of words in it—how none is inert or inactive or fails in its responsibility to the whole design. The theme of the poem has not the force or depth of Yeats' sonnet, and does not pretend to it: it is the creation of an emotional mood, not of a philosophic concept. It is as substantially emotional as Empson's poem is substantially intellectual. But the whole treatment reminds us at once of

Coleridge's description of the working of the poetic process—the reduction of multiplicity of material into unity—
the modification of a series of impressions into a dominant
feeling. As such it leads us on to the further discussion
of the logic of the imagination.

CHAPTER 9

The Logic of the Imagination

> . . . any obscurity of the poem, on first readings,
> is due to the suppression of "links in the chain," of
> explanatory and connecting matter, and not to in-
> coherence, or to the love of cryptogram. . . .
>   Such selection of a sequence of images and ideas
> has nothing chaotic about it. There is a logic of
> the imagination as well as a logic of concepts. Peo-
> ple who do not appreciate poetry always find it
> difficult to distinguish between order and chaos in
> the arrangement of images; and even those who
> are capable of appreciating poetry cannot always
> depend upon first impressions. I was not convinced
> of Mr Perse's imaginative order until I had read
> the poem five or six times. And if, as I suggest, such
> an arrangement of imagery requires just as much
> "fundamental brain-work" as the arrangement of an
> argument, it is to be expected that the reader of a
> poem should take at least as much trouble as a bar-
> rister reading an important decision on a compli-
> cated case.
>
> T. S. ELIOT. Preface to his translation
>   of *Anabase* by St. J. Perse.

'I HOPE Philosophy and Poetry will not neutralize
each other, and leave me an inert mass,' said Coleridge; and again, 'A whole essay might be written
on the danger of *thinking* without images.' Thinking in
images is imaginative logic, just as thinking in concepts
is intellectual logic. The essence of the logic of the imagination is that it can make abstractions concrete, by testing and interpreting them through the senses. Poetry is
the richest and most concentrated use of language because
it can fuse the abstract and the concrete, the intellectual

and the sensuous. When Hart Crane speaks of the sea as the 'wink of eternity,' he condenses into one image the suggestion of the momentary and the timeless; the actual physical gleam of the sea's surface, and the good humor of its mood. Or when Eliot describes the woman in *Gerontion* as 'poking the peevish gutter,' by an audacious ellipsis he compresses the sense of the negative uselessness of the woman's life, her obsession with unimportant material detail, and the emotional mood which colors her existence. In this way the logic of images is both an economy of language and an expansion of significance.

> Faun's flesh is not to us,
> Nor the saint's vision.
> We have the Press for wafer;
> Franchise for circumcision.

Here Pound does not *say* that political materialism has triumphed over myth and tradition, religion and ecstasy, but he presents the reader with a series of concrete images which evoke not only that one abstract concept, but a number of other ideas *and* sensuous suggestions. Auden does the same when he wishes to convey all the calm and security of a happy holiday with a friend:

> That later we, though parted then
> May still recall those evenings when
> Fear gave his watch no look;
> The lion griefs loped from the shade
> And on our knees their muzzles laid,
> And Death put down his book.

The poetry in these illustrations does not dispense with intellectual content, but it presents it in a different mode of perception: it unites the visionary with the visual.

§

Literature and human tradition are the great general
repositories of symbol and metaphor—immense stores of
emotive material which the poet can plunder at will. As
Yeats says: 'Whatever the passions of men have gathered
about becomes a symbol in the Great Memory, and, in
the hands of him that has the secret of it, a worker of
wonders, a caller up of angels or devils.' The memories
of all of us are stocked with such symbols. The emblems
of a watered valley, suggesting peace and well-being; of
the mountain peaks, suggesting aspiration; of wandering
in the darkness of corridors or caverns, suggesting frustration or the spiritual torment in the dim recesses of the individual soul; of wind, suggesting the spirit; of spring, the
song of the nightingale, the freshness of the rose, suggesting joy and beauty—all these, and many other common
symbols, have been enriched by centuries of literary use
and racial memory. When Eliot, for example, writes,

> Footfalls echo in the memory
> Down the passage which we did not take
> Towards the door we never opened
> Into the rose-garden

the mood of wistful regret for lost opportunities is immediately present to every reader.

But each age extends and modifies the area of association covered by the common memory. In the poetry of
today, for instance, it is inevitable that the world of
symbol and metaphor connected with the agricultural
basis of the old civilization and cosmogony should be
extended to include the urban, industrial and mechanical

worlds which have so largely replaced our traditional culture. Poets such as Auden, Empson and Day Lewis build up their poetic worlds with images drawn from mathematical physics, the internal-combustion engine or the vocabulary of psychoanalysis as naturally as the older poets spoke of a pair of compasses, the plow or the pit of despair. George Barker, in a poem on Rilke, links mysticism with physics, describing Rilke's 'X-ray gaze,' and how angels spoke to him 'opening their television bosoms'; or Dylan Thomas writes, 'The force that through the green fuse drives the flower,' uniting the old natural energies and the new mechanical energies in a single image. Thus the poet refreshes the language by new imagery, and releases the life of his own day into the life of his verse.

§

In addition to symbols and metaphors which are available to the poet in the common field of reference, some poets establish certain symbols personal to themselves which are focuses of association for their own experience. Blake is an illustration from the past, but there are many illustrations in the present age. The break with tradition and the rapid decay of a central cultural heritage have caused a shrinking and shriveling of that common stock of familiar metaphorical material to which both poet and reader instinctively respond.

Nightingales, Anangke, a sunset or the meanest flower
Were formerly the potentialities of poetry,
But now what have they to do with one another
With Dionysus or with me?

The old emblems are faded and the new have none of the warmth of long tradition or human attachment:

> they are not bred
> Flesh of our flesh, being unrelated
> Experientially, fused in no emotive furnace.*

Hence the poet feels the need of forging symbols of his own, or even uses completely private associations in the interests of psychological truth. Much of the obscurity of the modern arises from this. For a private symbolism, even if it is consistent, has to be established freshly in the mind of every reader, with no help from the past, and until the reader is familiar with the images and references, his understanding of the poetry is inhibited. In the last lines of *Byzantium*, for instance, unless the reader recognizes the group of concepts symbolized by Yeats in his use of the words 'gong' and 'dolphin,' the description of the sense-world as 'That dolphin-torn, that gong-tormented sea' loses its force. The poetry of Yeats or of Eliot has to be studied deeply, read and reread, before we become in any way at home with their personal symbolism—and its developments. For just as a great poetic artist in his use of past myths will always add something of his own to his material—as Yeats does to the Leda myth, or Eliot to the story of Marina—so he continues to add significance to his creation of his own personal symbols. Eliot's figures of drought or old age or gulls and the sea, for instance, though they remain constant, become incrusted with further deposits of meaning and expanded implications as he uses them in the course of his poetic practice; so do Yeats' symbols of the bobbin and the

* Ronald Bottrall. *The Thyrsis Retipped.*

mummy-cloth, the gyre and the swan. Indeed, we can soon recognize the difference in depth and quality between the poets who succeed in establishing this genuine, if obscure, calligraphy of symbol, and those whose attempts remain empty and arbitrary.

Hart Crane, for example, used a wilderness of imagery based largely on patterns of private association, which he failed to develop into any terms of permanent reference, and which lacks any germinal quality. He was constantly extending his range of metaphor, but he never intensified and enriched it with any accretions of meaning. And when he chose ready-made symbols, like Brooklyn Bridge and Pocahontas, he failed to endow them with the personal imaginative quality which would give them independent life. They remain superficial and rather commonplace symbols of transition and romance.

But apart from the use of large symbols, old and new, in the general body of a poet's works, there is the question of the way in which the logic of the imagination works in individual poems. Every poet, as we have seen, works in images, since all language is itself metaphorical, and the discovery, arrangement and development of images is of the essence of poetry. In the spontaneous intuition and the deliberate skill with which he builds up the structure of his imaginative logic we sense the quality of the poet. For there are as many pitfalls in the process of thinking in images as there are in the process of intellectual logic. In Empson's *Legal Fiction* we saw that metaphors can be precise and concise almost to a fault, so rigidly consistent in their pressure that they restrict the free emotional movement of the reader's apprehension. In *Euclid Alone Has Looked on Beauty Bare*, on the other hand, the images, instead of concentrating the experience, dissipate it. They have no vital relationship to one another: they are a heap, not a structure.

Again, a poet may be wasteful with his metaphors, squandering his substance. When Day Lewis writes:

> Others, too, will die hard,
> Spenders of life, they dealt freely with danger;
> These could not learn to hoard
> To count the cost or to examine the change.
> A hungry soul
> Urged them to try new air-routes, and their skill
> Raftered the sky with steel:
> They took the field with laughter, they attacked the
> 　bowling,

he is really adding very little by illustrating the statement in the first two lines in three different ways. But when Eliot makes Mr. Prufrock say, 'I have measured out my life with coffee spoons,' he telescopes in one image two complete ideas: that of partaking of life in tiny sips instead of delighting in its full flow and volume, and that of frittering it away in the sort of human and intellectual society symbolized by parties where

> the women come and go
> Talking of Michelangelo.

The mere association of things, the mere clashing of symbols, does not, of itself, have poetic value. 'All thought is sorting,' says I. A. Richards, and the test of the poet's achievement is the result of that process. It might be possible, indeed, to transpose Coleridge's remark quoted at the beginning of the chapter, and to say that a whole essay might be written about the danger of image-making without thinking, or the danger of relying for effects solely on the wealth of responses to experience which the human consciousness intuitively makes. The material of poetry, it is true, is rarely simple. As Eliot said, a reading of Spinoza, and the noise of the typewriter and the smell of dinner cooking may be all essential parts of a moment's experience. The poet, he reminds us, must look into a good deal more than the heart: he must look into the cerebral cortex, the nervous system and the digestive tract. But he does not take everything he finds there as of equal value. He 'sorts' it. And the problem before the critic is not the noting of the material present in the poet's consciousness, but the noting of what emerges from the sorting process. For, unlike logical argument, a poem is never the sum total of its individual features. It is a matter of the relationship among its images and statements; of the way they color and kindle and modify one another by the strategy of the poet's arrangement.

§

This arrangement may be a simple placing of one thing against another by way of contrast:

Consider this and in our time
As the hawk sees it or the helmeted airman . . .
Pass on, admire the view of the massif
Through plate-glass windows of the Sport Hotel;
Join there the insufficient units
Dangerous, easy, in furs, in uniform
And constellated at reserved tables
Supplied with feelings by an efficient band

> Relayed elsewhere to farmers and their dogs
> Sitting in kitchens in the stormy fens.*

Or again, instead of simple effects of this kind, the poet may build up a very complex and subtle effect by his juxtapositions. Eliot is particularly skillful in this way:

> At the violet hour, the evening hour that strives
> Homeward, and brings the sailor home from sea,
> The typist home at teatime, clears her breakfast, lights
> Her stove, and lays out food in tins.
> Out of the window perilously spread
> Her drying combinations touched by the sun's last rays. . . .

Here, without any statement or direct explanation, romance and realism, beauty and ugliness, tradition and actuality, past and present, are apprehended by a series of images whose associations in the reader's mind expand the meaning far beyond the actual words. 'The violet hour' suggests all the dim beauty of sunset and purple hills; the hour 'that strives homeward,' the double idea of the work that lies behind and the anticipated peace and relaxation of home; while the phrase 'the sailor home from sea' calls up not only the joy of all home-coming from long journeyings, but brings the verses of R. L. Stevenson to mind, with the further implication of the final rest of the grave after a fully lived life—of glad living and glad dying. Then from this, the mind is violently wrenched to a completely different vision—the vision of what 'home' is to the tired, slovenly typist, clearing her breakfast things at teatime, lighting her cheerless gas fire, eating out of tins; while the sun's last rays touch, not the violet hills, not the sea,

* W. H. Auden.

not the cosiness and welcome of a fireside peace, but her drying underclothes. Against memories of beauty and security and poetry, we have all the cheapness and the poverty and the unappetizing aspects of modern workers' civilization.

An illustration of a less successful creation of complex images may be seen in *The Emperor of Ice Cream*, by Wallace Stevens.

The theme of the contrast between reality and the imagination is a favorite one with Stevens. In *Another Weeping Woman*, speaking of the death which the loss of a loved one brings to the living, he writes:

> The magnificent cause of being,
> The imagination, the one reality
> In this imagined world
>
> Leaves you
> With him for whom no phantasy moves,
> And you are pierced by a death.

The 'phantasy' of the man of imagination, his mode of vision and its contrast and conflict with the perception of the plain facts of life, and the effort of the artist to bring them into some sort of relationship without distorting either, is the subject matter of *The Man with the Blue Guitar* and *Owl's Clover*. *The Emperor of Ice Cream* is a facet of this theme seen in a particular mood:

> Call the roller of big cigars,
> The muscular one, and bid him whip
> In kitchen cups concupiscent curds.
> Let the wenches dawdle in such dress
> As they are used to wear, and let the boys
> Bring flowers in last month's newspapers.

Let be be finale of seem.
The only emperor is the emperor of ice-cream.

Take from the dresser of deal,
Lacking the three glass knobs, that sheet
On which she embroidered fantails once
And spread it so as to cover her face.
If her horny feet protrude, they come
To show how cold she is, and dumb.
Let the lamp affix its beam.
The only emperor is the emperor of ice-cream.

Here the poet seems to have decided to view things 'exactly as they are.' Let us look at life, he says, without the imagination, 'Let be be finale of seem.' If we do this, the ruler of existence appears to be a materialistic force, an embodiment of human greed and pleasure-seeking, suitably symbolized by ice-cream. The death scene in the poem, therefore, is the final reality, stripped of all fantasy. Look at it steadily and clearly, 'Let the lamp affix its beam'; realize that there is no majesty in death; there is no mystery and tragic terror surrounding his court; his presence is just an excuse for a party. Don't let's pretend it is anything else; let the girls wear their ordinary clothes, not mourning; let the boys bring faded flowers, and send for the commonplace, muscular cigar-maker to come in and prepare some appetizing food. Don't trouble about any dignity or respect towards the dead woman's body. If the sheet doesn't cover her feet, what matter?—she can't object to anything.

Any criticism that may be brought against this poem is not as to the validity of the mood in which Stevens has conceived it, but to its success as an imaginative creation of that mood. The sense in which Stevens uses the word 'imagination' will be seen to be somewhat different from that of Coleridge. Instead of seeing the imagination as the power which controls *all* poetic material, he appears to equate it with 'fantasy,' emphasizing thereby the strange and dreamlike quality of the poetic vision. And indeed his own 'ecstasy' is apt to be of that nature: it has a strong element of the grotesque in it. But it is on the score of the 'shaping' power of the imagination, on the character of the arrangement of his fantastic images, that the poem fails of complete success. It is perhaps a weakness of Stevens' work as a whole that it is inclined to pass too often from the imaginative to the merely fanciful. The fanciful is quite in keeping with the mood of many of his poems, but not with the mood of this one, where the substance is gravely, even grimly, ironic. In his introduction to the poems of William Carlos Williams, he writes: 'Something of the unreal is necessary to fecundate the real; something of the sentimental to fecundate the anti-poetic.' This is very true, and, as we have seen, it is one of the attributes of the imaginative vision that it can subdue to the dominating mood of the poem the most unlikely and seemingly recalcitrant material, and harmonize the most apparent discords. But the harmonizing power must be there. If an image, by its oddity of association, obstinately refuses to submit to the dominion of its overlord, it may overset the poise of the whole poem, it may interrupt its emotional rhythm and flag the train. And it may well be argued that the epithet 'concupiscent' does that here. True, the derivation of the word signifies merely desire in general, but it is so commonly restricted to the sense of sexual desire that it hardly permits of any other suggestion. In the context, it provides surprise, and with a little help it can be made to carry a certain ironic overtone, by a reference to the sort of life the emperor of ice-cream presides over, and the revulsion we feel at its intrusion in the presence of death. The word is certainly 'something of the unreal' appearing as it does here. But it sterilizes rather than fecundates. Its strangeness and unexpectedness, so early in the poem, give it altogether too much weight, and the equilibrium of the mood is shaken by it. The rest of the stanza moves uncertainly, especially as the image of the flowers 'in last month's newspapers' is not a very happy one. It is the staleness of the flowers, not of the newspapers, which needs the accent.

It is not until the second stanza, with the straight, dry actuality of its opening lines, and the hard, clear image in the succeeding lines, that the original intention manifests itself and is triumphantly established. Indeed, Coleridge's distinction between the fancy and the imagination might be illustrated by the 'coming' of the dead woman's feet in this stanza, and the 'concupiscent curds' in the first. The function of the fanciful is the function of decoration: it is imposed upon the essential structure, which, if in just relation to it, it embellishes. But it is otherwise with imaginative effects. They are a living part of the structure. The expression 'concupiscent curds' performs, with some strain, a small function of ironic suggestion, but at the cost of diffusing the attention—like a wry, superior pleasantry which detracts more than it contributes. But the couplet

If her horny feet protrude, they come
To show how cold she is, and dumb

functions deeply within the body of the poem. Here the 'unreal' fecundates the real. Once the appearance of those feet would have sent the 'dawdling' mourners packing, but now they 'come' merely to show how helpless she is to rebuke the violators of the simplicity and frugality in which she lived. The physical picture of the 'real,' in all its raw ugliness, is vividly in keeping with the spirit of the poem, and the 'unreal' suggested in the 'coming' of the feet grows out of the real, and remains part of it, so that they fuse into an imaginative moment of great intensity. And the ironic contrast between the living and the dead woman is the subtle one of feeling, and is quite independent of mere strangeness of word association.

CHAPTER 10

Pattern

> That sentences in Authors, like haires in a horse-
> taile concurre in one roote of beauty and strength,
> but being pluckt out one by one, serve only for
> springes and snares.
>
> JOHN DONNE. *Newes From The Very Countrey*

WE have said in an earlier chapter that the first aim of the reader in examining a poem is to sense the mood which dominates it and then to explore the means by which the poet has given body and outline to that attitude. 'Ecstasy affords the occasion and expediency determines the form.'

The form is the pattern. As Eliot says: 'It is not our feelings, but the pattern we make of our feelings which is the centre of value.' It is twofold—the pattern of image and the pattern of sound—and its purpose is to subserve the theme of the poem through a subtle internal guidance of eye and ear. The theme and mood of the poem are revealed and interpreted in the pattern. This is not merely a decorative and harmonious arrangement: it is a structural directive. But it must be efficient without being assertive: it is servant, not master. The poem is the pattern, but the pattern is not the poem. In the poetry of E. E. Cummings, for instance, the patterns are often extremely interesting as experiments, but because they become overassertive, they soon lose their freshness and significance. They do not support anything *within* the poem, but function

merely as an isolated typographical caprice. Cummings'
tastes as a painter, too, make him overemphasize his image
pattern, so that his pattern is often little more than that.

> Picasso
> you give us Things
> which
> bulge

Auditory and visual pattern should complement one another and enforce one another. As a small example, when
Marianne Moore writes,

> Trying to open locked doors with a sword, threading
> the points of needles, planting shade trees
> upside down,

the image pattern, suggestive of effort and frustration,
directs the reading to a heavy stress on the first syllables
of 'trying,' 'threading,' 'planting,' while the recoil in the
final syllable completes the sense impression. It is a perfect
marriage of image and sound.

§

The whole trend of modern poetry has been towards
emphasis on pattern value and the subtilizing of it. Edith
Sitwell, discussing the character and significance of poetic
structure at various periods, finds a sistership in the Au-
gustan age between poetry and architecture, and in the
romantic age between poetry and music. Now she sees
poetry as the sister of horticulture, 'Each poem growing
according to the laws of its own nature, but in a line which
is more often the irregular though entirely natural shape
of a tree or a flowering plant.' Laura Riding and Robert

Graves, in their *Survey of Modernist Poetry*, insist on
this same irregularity—an irregularity which illustrates
not carelessness but natural vitality. 'The whole trend of
modern poetry is towards treating poetry like a very sensitive substance which succeeds better when allowed to
crystallize by itself than when put into prepared moulds."

This tendency towards formal irregularity is seen in
both image and sound pattern. It was called into being by
the new quality of experience sensed particularly by the
French Symbolists, and widely developed by contemporary English and American writers. A new image pattern was required which could convey both rapid changes
of feeling and a vivid realization of the complexity of the
human consciousness—the fact that divergent and conflicting experiences could be simultaneously present in the
poet's mind. The basis of this attitude was dramatic, not
reflective or descriptive; the experience itself was usually
fragmentary, not ordered; hence the predominating visual
design became that of the juxtaposition of concentrated
and often unconnected symbols. Its parallels in the visual
arts can be seen in Expressionist and Surrealist painting
and in the technique of the moving picture.

Its parallel in sound pattern was 'free verse.' The word
'pattern' carries with it usually a suggestion of regularity
and recurrence, and a long tradition has associated pattern in poetry with the use of regular meter and recur-
rent rhythm. But just as the Expressionist and Surrealist
painters proved that definite pattern may exist in painting
in the midst of formal irregularity, so the poets declared
that it could exist in words apart from traditional metrical
bonds. The new mode of experience found such tradi-

tional bonds a contradiction to its very spirit, and attempted to supersede them with the pliancy of arbitrary practice.

But as Eliot declared in a very interesting article on free verse,* the term itself is a misnomer, 'It is a battle cry of freedom, and there is no freedom in art.' He points out that there is never any escape from meter in poetry, there is only mastery of it; and that the division between free verse and conservative verse does not in fact exist: 'there is only good verse, bad verse, and chaos.'

We may therefore formulate as follows: the ghost of some simple metre should lurk behind the arras in even the 'freest' verse; to advance menacingly as we doze, and withdraw as we rouse. Or, freedom is only true freedom when it appears against the background of an artificial limitation.

'Not to have perceived the truth that *some* artificial limitation is necessary except in moments of the first intensity is, I believe, a capital error.'

And that indeed is the weakness in the sound pattern of much post-war poetry. The poet has his own ends, and is entitled to use whatever means, whatever kind of 'expediency,' he thinks will produce them; but a means which ignores the collaboration of a governing limitation seldom does produce them. If the sound pattern has no agreed-upon rhythm or shape of its own, it throws upon the poet the necessity of creating it freshly and vitally with every word he writes. A meter in itself concentrates attention and tends to stimulate sensibility, imposing a zone of necessity upon the poetic process. Without it, the force and flexibility of the poet's sensibilities must pro-

* *The New Statesman*, March 3, 1917.

vide the whole principle of flow, control and unification. It is as if a painter, instead of creating his pattern within the limits of a frame, should compose on a canvas whose outline should be an irregular arrangement of curves, angles, protuberances and indentations dictated by the free rhythms of his own mind. An illustration of the danger may be seen in the poetry of D. H. Lawrence, which often spreads like a stain instead of growing like a plant. But such freedom can communicate rich and original effects. A good example is the section of *The Bridge* called *Cutty Sark*. The chance encounter on the New York water front described in the opening lines overflows into a romantic reminiscence of clipper ships against the music of a mechanical piano. It is a frankly romantic piece, but Crane's technique of presentation has lessened the sentimental weakness which mars so much of the poem. His method is one of auditory imagery developed through the piano in the background 'Weaving somebody's nickel.' An atmosphere of fading and fusing sounds gradually emerges. 'Dreams weave' dissolves into 'drums weave' after 'his bony hands got to beating time,' which in turn fades into

                    —Heave, weave
    those bright designs the trade winds drive. . . .

Then the clipper ships appear as a romantic memory floating in a mist of echoed sounds:

                         Pennants, parabolas—
            baronial white on lucky blue!
                    .   .   .   .
        Perennial—*Cutty*—trophied—*Sark!*

'Pennants,' 'parabolas' and 'baronial' are fused into 'perennial,' which with its companion 'trophied' penetrates the identity of the ship by dividing the name.

Here the audacity of complete freedom is triumphant; but such a triumph is rare. A great poetic craftsman finds his source of energy more often in the dramatic possibilities of the conflict between the variations of emotional tone in his poem, of the images he employs to create these, and the technical demands of a metrical scheme. The effect of this in an elaborate stanza can be studied in Yeats' *Byzantium* or *Among School Children*, and Eliot's *Gerontion* illustrates the sense of tension and strength created by 'the ghost of a simple metre lurking behind the arras.' The 'ghost' is the blank verse of the later Elizabethans, and the poem ends with these lines:

These with a thousand small deliberations
Protract the profit of their chilled delirium,
Excite the membrane, when the sense has cooled,
With pungent sauces, multiply variety
In a wilderness of mirrors. What will the spider do,
Suspend its operations, will the weevil
Delay? De Bailhache, Fresca, Mrs. Cammel, whirled
Beyond the circuit of the shuddering Bear
In fractured atoms. Gull against the wind, in the windy
        straits
Of Belle Isle, or running on the Horn,
White feathers in the snow, the Gulf claims,
And an old man driven by the Trades
To a sleepy corner.

The poet is presenting, through the medium of a complex and concentrated series of images, the despairing realization of the restlessness which has replaced true vitality in modern civilization, and his premonition of its final collapse. He envisages the extinction of certain evil aspects of contemporary society, and the no less certain extinction of the feeble but courageous elements still existing. And he contemplates it helplessly. A dramatic effect is secured by the mutations of these moods and images, varieties in pace and texture of sound pattern. In addition, a contrapuntal effect is achieved by an opposition between these incidental dramatic variations and the underlying unity of sound pattern. This pattern is in itself varied by subtle evasions and advances, momentum and recoil; the poet takes the utmost liberties with it to suit his purpose, but it is always there, as an artificial limitation holding the whole in a frame.

§

Free unrhymed verse was not an invention of the present age. It had been practiced for some thousands of years, and reaches back to the incantation which linked verse with the ritual dance. It produced a communal emotion; the aim of the cadenced phrases was to create a state of mind. A great deal of verse still functions as incantation and appeals to the reader on that level. Eliot's often quoted description of the 'auditory imagination,' in his essay on Matthew Arnold, stresses this appeal. He is pointing out the limitations of Arnold's definition of poetry as a 'criticism of life,' and the profound influence of sound value in the reading of poetry:

What I call the 'auditory imagination' is the feeling for syllable and rhythm, penetrating far below the conscious levels of thought and feeling, invigorating every word;

sinking to the most primitive and forgotten, returning to the origin and bringing something back, seeking the beginning and the end. It works through meanings, certainly, and not without meanings in the ordinary sense, and fuses the old and obliterated and the trite, the current, and the new and surprising, the most ancient and the most civilized mentality.

The 'meaning,' apart from 'meanings in the ordinary sense,' which can be communicated in the workings of the auditory imagination are felt very powerfully in *Ash Wednesday*, where the whole tone and mood of the poem is established at once in the flow of syllable and rhythm, and makes itself known to the reader 'far below the conscious levels of thought and feeling' and without intellectual apprehension at all.

But the fact that *Ash Wednesday* is a poem of religious experience, that its quality is visionary and its music largely liturgical, is what gives it that dominant flavor of a ritual chant. The general coloring of free rhythms in the poetry of today is very different. The aim of Pound, and the Eliot of the early poems, was to reinstate the natural speech rhythm in poetic practice. This is the sharpest difference between the patterns of 'post-war' verse and the verse of the nineteenth and early twentieth centuries. In his introduction to the *Selected Poems of Ezra Pound*, Eliot makes a distinction between verse as *speech* and verse as *song*, and there is no question as to the category in which most modern verse belongs. Walter de la Mare is a poet of songs, and Yeats wrote much poetry of that type. Among the younger poets Auden, Eberhart, Prokosch and a few others have returned to it in snatches, but the predominant pattern of poetry today is that of speech rhythm. Pound urged the Imagists to compose in the sequence of the musical phrase, not in the sequence of the metronome, the regular beat, and it is he even more than Eliot who was responsible for the revolution which followed. But during the twenties, the practice of both Pound and Eliot hardened into a theory which dispensed with strict formality of sound pattern. Conventional rhyme fell into almost complete disuse. But here again Eliot pointed the way to further development. In the article from which we have already quoted, he states that it is true that excessive devotion to rhyme thickens the ear, and that in order to restore its sensibility an avoidance of rhyme may be very salutary. But he goes on to show that its general avoidance should sharpen its value in particular application:

This liberation from rhyme might be as well a liberation of rhyme. Freed of its exacting task of supporting lame verse, it could be applied with greater effect where it is most needed. There are often passages in an unrhymed poem where rhyme is wanted for some special effect, for a sudden tightening up, for a cumulative insistence, or for an abrupt change of mood.

Many such effects might be illustrated from Eliot's own work, but his general thesis that the liberation from rhyme might be a liberation of rhyme has been abundantly fulfilled. The break in the tradition of rhymed verse had the healthy effect of giving it a fresh start, released from the hampering convention of too familiar cadences—too familiar alike to writers and to readers. This freshening and subtilizing of the use of rhyme can be seen everywhere today, particularly in the blending of it with the new easy speech idiom. It may be in a muted sound pat-

tern of subdued internal rhyme combined with a flowing
natural rhythm, as in Horace Gregory's *What John Blue-
thorne Heard at the New Year*:

Now and tomorrow the danger is always here,
In quiet rooms the bird has left behind,
Like the unheard, unhearing echo of a sound
When no one says a word but sits awake, each still face
　　saying
To itself, We must have no more hysteria here. . . .

Or this ease and assurance of movement may accompany
a concentrated and elaborate rhyme scheme—a form in
which Yeats is particularly skillful:

　There is grey in your hair.
　Young men no longer suddenly catch their breath
　When you are passing;
　But maybe some old gaffer mutters a blessing
　Because it was your prayer
　Recovered him upon the bed of death.
　For your sole sake—that all heart's ache have known,
　And given to others all heart's ache,
　From meagre girlhood's putting on
　Burdensome beauty—for your sole sake
　Heaven has put away the stroke of her doom,
　So great her portion in that peace you make
　By merely walking in a room.*

Auden had returned to the ballad, with its positive and
assertive rhyme beat, but now seems to have discarded
that and to be working towards a wider and more 'lucid
song.' *Voltaire at Ferney* † shows him adopting a rhyming
method which, while very simple, is very cunning, and
has none of the monotony of the ballad chime. The end
variants of the first three stanzas prevent a too prepared

* *Broken Dreams.*
† See p. 104.

ear in the reader, while the uniformity of rhyme in the last three clinches the quiet decisiveness of tone and composes the ear for the reflectiveness and resolution of the conclusion. The majority of younger and less resourceful poets, however, fearing the obvious, have tended to avoid the full end rhyme, and poetic craftsmanship has been lavished on every subtlety of half rhyme and near rhyme, of internal and hidden rhyme, of the rhyming of unstressed syllables and the definite rhyme disappointment. Marianne Moore is perhaps the most deliberate and subtle craftsman of them all. With the return of rhyme has come the development of many fresh metrical devices as well as the revival of some of the Old English alliterative measures. The new emphasis on the fall of the phrase rather than on the beat of the metrical foot is seen everywhere. The most popular verse music is that of the irregular stress, not of the regular syllabic measure, and variety is given by the shifting of the caesura, or pause, and by the internal tactics of vowel modulation, assonance and alliteration.

§

These devices, in conjunction with an equal care in the management of visual pattern, have created a poetry of the most intricate craftsmanship. Enjoyment of such poetry does not depend upon an analysis of the poet's technical means, but it may be greatly increased by an understanding appreciation of them and of the exacting discipline behind the poet's work. For as Yeats said:

a line will take us hours maybe;
Yet if it does not seem a moment's thought,

Our stitching and unstitching has been naught.
Better go down upon your marrow-bones
And scrub a kitchen pavement, or break stones
Like an old pauper, in all kinds of weather;
For to articulate sweet sounds together
Is to work harder than all these, and yet
Be thought an idler by the noisy set
Of bankers, schoolmasters, and clergymen
The martyrs call the world.*

Let us take two poems where we can see something of
this 'stitching' and note its quality. First a poem by James
Agee, which illustrates a masterly integration of sound
and image pattern woven and interwoven within the
fabric of the verse:

Sunday: Outskirts of Knoxville, Tenn.

There, in the earliest and chary spring, the dogwood
    flowers.

Unharnessed in the friendly sunday air
By the red brambles, on the river bluffs,
Clerks and their choices pair.

Thrive by, not near, masked all away by shrub and ju-
    niper,
The ford v eight, racing the chevrolet.

They can not trouble her:

Her breasts, helped open from the afforded lace,
Lie like a peaceful lake;
And on his mouth she breaks her gentleness:

Oh, wave them awake!

They are not of the birds. Such innocence
Brings us to break us only.
Theirs are not happy words.

* *Adam's Curse.*

We that are human cannot hope.
Our tenderest joys oblige us most.
No chain so cuts the bone; and sweetest silk most
    shrewdly strangles.

How this must end, that now please love were ended,
In kitchens, bedfights, silences, women's-pages,
Sickness of heart before goldlettered doors,
Stale flesh, hard collars, agony in antiseptic corridors,
Spankings, remonstrances, fishing trips, orange juice,
Policies, incapacities, a chevrolet,
Scorn of their children, kind contempt exchanged,
Recalls, tears, second honeymoons, pity,
Shouted corrections of missed syllables,
Hot water bags, gallstones, falls down stairs,
Oldfashioned christmases, suspicions of theft,
Arrangements with morticians taken care of by sons in
    law,
Small rooms beneath the gables of brick bungalow,
The tumbler smashed, the glance between daughter and
    husband,
The empty body in the lonely bed
And, in the empty concrete porch, blown ash
Grandchildren wandering the betraying sun

Now, on the winsome crumbling shelves of the horror
God show, God blind these children!

The visual pattern opens with the lyric imagery of
rural courtship, then darkens its loveliness with negation
and pictures of pain, and finally projects the inventory
which unwinds with cinematic vividness and speed to
the end of life. In the plea of the last two lines the poem
is summarized. The moment of love in the opening passage is recalled by 'winsome,' and the empty shell of
sordidness to follow is suggested by the 'crumbling shelves
of horror,' an image reflecting the form in which the
inventory was stated.

The last line is the concentration of human pity in a prayer torn by the twofold vision of the poem. A prayer that the future may be disclosed to these unsuspecting 'children.' A prayer that God's pity may blind them to the future and allow them the beauty of that lyrical moment of love.

The sound pattern is handled with equal skill. Throughout the opening section down to the line

> Oh, wave them awake!

it is one of light lyrical emphasis and soft internal and end rhyme. The introductory rhymes fall on such sounds as 'there,' 'chary,' 'air,' 'pair,' 'earliest' and 'clerk.' Then the soft 'r' sound subsides and the long 'a' sound first suggested in 'away' and 'chevrolet' reasserts itself in a sharper form, gradually developing from the smoothness of this sound in 'lace' to its sharpness in 'awake.' On this word the first movement ends, and the note of pity is introduced. But the sound pattern at this point develops directly from the word 'awake' through its long 'a' echo in the introductory word 'They.' The soft 'r' sounds of the opening lines reappear but now in a more compressed and rigid form and shaded by sharp negatives. These two verses are constructed in a pattern of monosyllabic key words, direct and sharp as the key line,

> Oh, wave them awake!

Whereas 'wave' and 'awake' are echoed in the initial word 'They,' which is the point of emphasis at this juncture, the sound of 'Oh' is echoed in the rhymes of the stanza:

> We that are human cannot hope.
> Our tenderest joys oblige us most.

No chain so cuts the bone; and sweetest silk most
shrewdly strangles.

And the monosyllabic sound is hardened and carried over
into the opening lines of the inventory which echoes in
its first word the sound of 'flowers' in the first line of the
poem—

How this must end, that now please love were ended.

This line, with its clean, internal rhyme, is a verse in itself structurally contrasted with the tumbling variety
of the inventory which follows. Here, the sound pattern
recedes into a monotone supported by irregular rhymes
like shelves of cliff descending brokenly into an abyss:

The tumbler smashed, the glance between daughter and
husband
The empty body in the lonely bed
And, in the empty concrete porch, blown ash
Grandchildren wandering the betraying sun

The content of these lines is the end of life, and the sound
pattern tightens around it with internal echoes and rhymes
between 'smashed' and 'ash,' 'lonely' and 'blown,' 'tumbler,' 'sun' and 'husband' and the significant repetition
of 'empty.' The two final lines of the poem open with the
sound which introduces the inventory. Again the sound
of 'flowers' from the first line is echoed. And in the words
'crumbling' and 'children' are echoed the first and last
sounds of the closing line of the inventory. Thus the
sound pattern is preserved intact and retained within the
poem, always ancillary to the visual pattern; and by means
of his organization the poet is enabled to shuttle back-
ward and forward across his theme, controlling the read-

er's response by suggestion rather than by statement, establishing fresh juxtapositions of symbols and images already used without resorting to restatement or duplication of means. Agee's poem is a superlative example of the effectiveness of pattern in these respects. Throughout, we are kept constantly aware of the two visions which compose the poem. The idyllic vision persists within the shadow of the realistic vision until the closing prayer brackets both. This dual vision is not sustained by means of direct reference but always by means of suggestion within the visual or sound pattern—a method which recalls Mallarmé's acknowledged aim, 'to evoke an object in deliberate shadow without ever actually mentioning it, by allusive words, never by direct words.'

Les Sylphides, by Louis MacNeice, presents a different treatment of a theme similar to that of Agee's poem. The difference is evident not only in tone and attitude but also in pattern:

Les Sylphides

Life in a day: he took his girl to the ballet,
Being short-sighted himself could hardly see it—
    The white skirts in the grey
    Glade and the swell of the music
    Lifting the white sails.

Calyx upon calyx, Canterbury bells in the breeze,
The flowers on the left mirror to the flowers on the right
    And the naked arms above
    The powdered faces moving
    Like seaweed in a pool.

Now, he thought, we are floating—ageless, oarless—
Now there is no separation, from now on
    You will be wearing white

Satin and a red sash
Under the waltzing trees.

But the music stopped, the dancers took their curtain,
The river had come to a lock—a shuffle of programmes—
  And we cannot continue down
  Stream unless we are ready
  To enter the lock and drop.

So they were married—to be the more together—
And found they were never again so much together,
  Divided by the morning tea,
  By the evening paper,
  By children and tradesmen's bills.

Waking at times in the night she found assurance
In his regular breathing but wondered whether
  It was really worth it and where
  The river had flowed away
  And where were the white flowers.

This poem being an expression of disillusion, its pattern is adjusted to the expression so that there is an emphasis on the idyllic vision, whereas in Agee's poem the realistic vision is emphasized with the idyllic vision carried always in close proximity to it. For the source of the pity expressed in Agee's poem is the contrast and *balance* between the two visions. The source of the disillusion and disappointment in MacNeice's poem is the contrast and *unbalance* between the two visions. In disillusion and disappointment the memory of past happiness dominates the contrast. In the pity of Agee's poem both visions are deeply and fully considered. In MacNeice's poem division and not unity is realized in marriage. The fact is briefly stated. The situation is accepted with misgiving and regrets. The last two lines of the poem recall by restatement the imagery of the idyll. The plight described does not plead for pity. It is regrettable but not unusual to suffer disillusion. And here there is at least a very clear memory of happiness. In the last lines of Agee's poem there is no statement *directly* recalling the moment of happiness. There is no clear memory of happiness at this point. It is indistinct and almost forgotten. So Agee recalls it not by restatement of the symbol, as in *Les Sylphides*, but by the word 'winsome' which qualifies 'crumbling shelves of horror' in such a way that the two visions become fused in the final prayer. Had MacNeice employed such a subdued method of recall in his pattern the expression of disillusion would have been diminished in impact. The force of the expression lies in the clarity with which the expectation of happiness is remembered. By the same token had Agee directly restated a symbol from his opening lines (the dogwood or red brambles) the effect would have been much less poignant and the ambivalence of the prayer less justifiable. The suggestion that the idyllic memory will be almost entirely erased by the painful years which follow justifies the prayer for revelation. But in recalling the idyll by one faintly allusive word the poet reminds us of the actual happiness which justifies the counterplea that knowledge of the future be withheld.

And in *Les Sylphides* as in Agee's poem the sound pattern plays its part in the effect achieved. For in the final stanza there is a return to the long 'a' and sharp 'i' sounds which are so conspicuous in the first three stanzas. Thus the sound pattern assists in reviving the vision which is the chief source of the poet's theme.

In the work of many minor poets of today, it must be
owned that all this extremely intricate craftsmanship appears very often as an overelaborate prelude to a somewhat slim content. The interest of technical devices is
not in themselves but in what they reveal: the poem is
the pattern, but the pattern is not the poem. The exciting
thing about a poet is not so much his mastery of technique
as his power apparently to transcend technique in the true
arrogance of inspiration—to stretch, contract or distort
his medium to reveal an individual and compelling rhythm;
to achieve what Flaubert calls 'those thrusts of power
beyond the reach of conscious art.' Many of the poets of
the last twenty years have been verbal gymnasts, exercis-
ing themselves in feats of dexterity, giving displays of
virtuosity and ingenuity which we may watch with admiration, but which seem to lead to very little and to
be ends in themselves. Yet the preoccupation with craft
is a healthy sign in poetry. Without craft there is no art.
Matthew Arnold, at the conclusion of the Preface to his
own poetry, quotes Goethe as saying that there are two
kinds of dilettanti in poetry: 'he who neglects the indis-
pensable mechanical part, and thinks he has done enough
if he shows spirituality and feeling; and he who seeks to
arrive at poetry merely by mechanism, in which he can
acquire an artisan's readiness, and is without the soul of
the matter.' Goethe says that the first does most harm to
art, and the latter to himself. Arnold's comment is:

If we must be *dilettanti:* if it is impossible for us, under
the circumstances amidst which we live, to think clearly,
to feel nobly, and to delineate firmly: if we cannot attain
to the mastery of the great artists—let us at least have so

much respect for our Art as to prefer it to ourselves: let us not bewilder our successors: let us transmit to them the practice of Poetry, with its boundaries and wholesome regulative laws, under which excellent works may again, perhaps at some future time, be produced, not yet fallen into oblivion through our neglect, nor yet condemned and cancelled by the influence of their eternal enemy, Caprice.

CHAPTER 11

The Poet's Tongue

And from the first declension of the flesh
I learnt man's tongue, to twist the shapes of thoughts
Into the stony idiom of the brain,
To shade and knit anew the patch of words
Left by the dead who, in their moonless acre,
Need no word's warmth.

DYLAN THOMAS

THE history of language owes, perhaps, more to the poet than to any other single agent. Language is like the fertile surface of the earth, a soil subject to erosion, whose fecundity is constantly threatened by elements which destroy its vitality and impoverish its content. Time washes away its surface freshness, and use exhausts its fertility; unless it is constantly invigorated and fructified by due nourishment, it becomes arid and sterile. And as the character of a country can be seen in its soil, so the consciousness of an age is revealed in its speech. Poetry, since it is the most concentrated and comprehensive use of speech, holds within itself the power both to remint the old worn coinage of traditional expression, and to issue new currency. Poetry is words. The poet, in spite of Donne, is never 'a naked thinking heart that makes no show'; he is Keats writing his first letter to Fanny Brawne, 'I want a brighter word than bright, a fairer word than fair.'

As the poetic tradition of any age wears itself out and

degenerates into formalism and mechanical imitation, the poet with the pressure of a new vitality within him will inevitably find a new speech. This need not necessarily be a speech colored with contemporary idiom, but it will be a reflection of the modes of thought and feeling which have called it into being. The verbal rhythms of *Gerontion*, for instance, are those of Jacobean drama, but the emotion they transmit is as modern as that suggested by the Impressionist notation and advertising slogans of Cummings or Williams, which already appear a little faded. Indeed, anything very obviously 'up to date' in language is apt to be ephemeral. Nowadays we find the literary and emotional poses of the nineties quaint and a little florid:

> I have forgot much, Cynara! Gone with the wind,
> Flung roses, roses, riotously with the throng,
> Dancing to put thy pale lost lilies out of mind.

And maybe the next generation will find our version of the same thing equally quaint and a little artificial:

I . . . have stuttered on my feet
Clinched to the streamlined and butter smooth trulls of
    the élite.

For it is not a language reflecting the superficial veneer of contemporary science and society which makes a poet significant, but a mind which has digested and assimilated both past and present, and emerges in an invigorated idiom possessing new blood and breath.

§

The basic difference between words as used in poetry and in prose is the *amount of activity* which they assume.

Wordsworth declared that 'the language of a large portion of every good poem even of the most elevated character, must necessarily in no respect differ from that of
good prose.' This is true. The good prose writer does
not waste words, and he uses them with a keen eye to
their balance, rhythm, texture and sound. But the poet has
to work in a narrower compass, and he must therefore
exercise more particular and precise qualities of compression and design.

Yeats said of Henley: 'Half his opinions were the contrivance of a subconscious that sought always to bring
. . . expression to that point of artifice where the true
self could find its tongue.' It is to that point of artifice
where the true self can find its tongue that the poet seeks
to bring his expression. It is a curious, seemingly para-
doxical conjunction of ideas, this one which associates
artifice of expression with the tongue of the poet's true
self. Usually we think of artifice and truth as in opposition. Actually it is not so. By grinding, a lens is brought to
the point of artifice at which true vision is communicated
to the eye. By a process similar to grinding, expression
is brought to that point of artifice at which the poet's
true self is communicated to his tongue, or translated
into speech. The grinding process is described by Yeats
as the 'stitching and unstitching' by which a line which
seems but a moment's thought may take the poet hours
to write.

And the basic 'contrivance' of the poet is his use of
words. By the value of his words we assess him as a poet.
This does not mean that it is mere wealth or facility of

word usage that we look for. There is a verbal high spirits, which expresses itself in letting language run wild, turn somersaults or play leapfrog, and which is often attractive. We can see illustrations in Edith Sitwell's breathless doggerel verses, or the good fun of Cummings. Or there is that capacity to invent new words containing fusions of meaning within them, which we associate particularly with James Joyce, but which we find so often in Hopkins, or among modern poets, in Eugène Jolas. But the real technical artifice of the poet is seen in the values—meaning value, image value, sound value—with which he can charge his language.

A single word may be at once the intellectual and emotional pivot of a poem and its musical motif, thus dominating its complete rhythm. In Canto XLV, the wickedness and horror which Pound feels to be rooted in usury is summed up in a poem of fifty lines, where the word *usura* occurs twenty times. Avoiding argument or censure, Pound uses an effect of incantation which is very powerful:

> Stone cutter is kept from his stone
> weaver is kept from his loom
> WITH USURA
> wool comes not to market
> sheep bringeth no gain with usura
> Usura is a murrain, usura
> blunteth the needle in the maid's hand
> and stoppeth the spinner's cunning.

The use of the Latin term, with its plenum of religious and historical associations, insures a singleness of significance for the word, which the modern 'usury' would not have. And this word *usura* moves back and forth through the phrasing like a color in the loom or a theme in a musical composition, so that it supports the whole rhythm of the poem.

Or again, a perfectly simple word may develop a tremendous evocative power from the position in which it appears:

> How can those terrified vague fingers push
> The feathered glory from her loosening thighs?

The sense of gradually diminishing resistance and willing surrender is achieved here by surrounding the small precise word 'push' with words of much greater emotional content and scope. The effort of resistance qualified in this way becomes slight, almost perfunctory, and the poet thus invents a special meaning for the word which corresponds exactly to the situation. Again, a poet may modify the accepted connotation of a word by using it in a new setting, and so giving it a new value: 'the abating shadow of our *conscript* dust'; juxtaposition of words may blend and alter their coloring and significance, the abstract enlarging the concrete, the concrete vitalizing the abstract: 'withered stumps of time,' 'the fury and the mire of human veins'; an ambiguity of meaning may give a double interest and a wider interpretation:

> What will the spider do,
> Suspend its operations . . . ?

Perfectly commonplace words may take on poetic value by the movement of a line: 'Easily, my dear, you move your head,' and a complete platitude may stir us profoundly by the words in which it is expressed:

An aged man is but a paltry thing,
A tattered coat upon a stick, unless
Soul clap its hands and sing . . .

Poets differ very widely, however, in the amount of work they make words do, the amount of activity they inject into them. The great poet like Shakespeare appears unconsciously to use every value which can be wrung from his medium. Music, meaning, memory; simplicity and ornament; visual image and abstract idea; dramatic force and lyric intensity; direct statement and oblique suggestion; color, light, power, are distilled from the whole mass of language into the spirit of poetry. His words are alive in every part of their being—body, mind and heart. Lesser poets tend to emphasize certain potentialities of words and to ignore others.

Among modern poets, Crane exploits sound and emotional tone, largely ignoring the logical content of words; Marianne Moore accents delicacy of cadence and 'neatness of finish,' with the emphasis on the precision and the patina of language rather than on its suggestiveness, its capacity for 'tolling reminiscent bells.' Cummings is partial to a personal calligraphy. Hence eccentricity dominates his vocabulary, and interspersed with vivid original epithets we read of a face 'clinched in a swoon of synopsis,' or of 'the sumptuous screech of simplicity.' Wallace Stevens in his early poems illustrates the same bent towards a private poetic world abounding in oddness and preciosity, 'prinking' it in 'bright chromes,' 'dithery gold' and 'musky muscadines.'

There is, further, the division of poets into intuitive poets and deliberate poets. It represents a real temperamental cleavage. This is seen at its most obvious in the difference between Shakespeare and Milton, or Browning and Tennyson, or Yeats and Pound, but it runs through the whole history of poetry. In the present day, poets such as Hart Crane, Dylan Thomas and Richard Eberhart are intuitive poets. They may disappoint as often as they satisfy; they have an inconsistent quality which makes their success often precarious, but such lines as

> The seal's wide spindrift gaze towards paradise,

or

> O see the pulse of summer in the ice,

or

> And ever and still the weight of mystery
> Arrows a way between my words and me

have a direct inevitability which is the unmistakable voice of intuitive rhythmic compulsion. Poets such as Marianne Moore, Stephen Spender and F. T. Prince, on the other hand, are deliberate poets. It is not so much the stimulating shock, the 'sudden blood,' which affects us, but rather the enjoyment of fastidious workmanship:

To a Man on His Horse

> Only the Arab stallion will I
> Envy you. Along the water
> You dance him with the morning on his flanks.
> In the frosty morning that his motions flatter
> He kindles and where the winter's in the wood
> I watch you dance him out on delicate shanks.
> And lashes fall on a dark eye,
> He sheds a silvery mane, he shapes
> His thin nostrils like a fop's.

And to do honour to his whiteness
In remembrance of his ancient blood
I have wished to become his groom
And so his smouldering body comb
In a simple and indecorous sweetness.*

And as the uses of poetic language differ in individual
poets, so there are marked differences in their use in
various cultural epochs. The Augustans use language
almost entirely in its logical sense, gaining their effects
by concentration and economy of means; the romantics
specialized in sensuous effects, using words particularly
for their pictorial and musical value; the Victorians loved
rhetoric and the large vague emotional appeal.

The characteristic contemporary use of words differs
from all these. If we look for any parallel in the past, it
is in the seventeenth century Metaphysicals. That age
too followed an age of great positive creative activity,
and it has certain of the same peculiarities as our own. It
was an age of 'private' poetry, when the lyric dominated
all other poetic forms, and when the poet's vocabulary
sprang not so much from the nature of the experience
which was his material, as from the nature of his own
intensely personal response to it. The distinction between
the love poetry of *Romeo and Juliet* and that of Donne's
Songs and Sonnets, or that between Browning's *Andrea
del Sarto* and Eliot's *Prufrock* will point the difference.
In an age of weakened cultural traditions the poet no
longer sees experience within a large coherent outline
which can be interpreted in solid dramatic or narrative

* F. T. Prince.

form. He concentrates instead on the particular moment, the personal mood—on what may be called the lyric mode of vision.

The qualities which the lyric mode of experience particularly emphasize are those of concentration and singularity. The driving forces behind the poet are the urge to reveal the complexity of his experience and to accent its personal flavor. In an age when the richer and fuller experiences of the artist's vision naturally reflect themselves in narrative or dramatic poetry, the lyric is apt to take the form of light and graceful song, as it did in the early Elizabethan age; or of simple or decorative verses, as it did with the Victorians. But in the present day the lyric has had to reveal the whole content of the poet's mind, his whole response to living. The result is that words have had to work harder than they have ever worked before as an interpretative medium, and that there has been an absorption in the craft of conveying the utmost density of consciousness in the smallest possible compass of language.

One aspect of this bent towards economy of means is seen in the extreme compression of modern poetic syntax. The influence of Gerard Manley Hopkins had much to do with this. In his poetry the omission of article and relative pronoun, the substitution of one part of speech for another, sentence inversions and elliptical constructions all play a part in communicating his closely woven texture of thought and feeling. There are traces of this influence in Auden's early poems:

Bones wrenched, weak whimper, lids wrinkled, first dazzle known,

World-wonder hardened as bigness, years, brought knowl-
   edge, you:
Presence a rich mould augured for roots urged—but gone
The soul is tetanous. . . .

Wyndham Lewis describes this technique:

I sabotage the sentence! With me is the naked word.
I spike the verb—all parts of speech are pushed over on
   their backs.
I am the master of all that is half-uttered and imperfectly
   heard.
Return with me where I am crying out with the gorilla
   and the bird.

It was all part of the effort to eliminate everything
which was not directly serviceable. Another illustration
of it is the fondness of some poets for effects based literally on the 'naked word'—the value to be obtained from
the precise catalogue of objects which, though it appears
at first sight to be mere summation, is in reality a method
of obtaining a maximum concentration of pregnant matter.
The twelfth line of *Gerontion*, for instance, runs:

> Rocks, moss, stonecrop, iron, merds.

The poet has been using a series of images to present his
picture of modern civilization. Then he interrupts the
pictures, and the active rhythm in which they have been
moving, with this line of heavily stressed single words.
The reader is forced to pause, jerked by the change in the
rhythm into attention to these insistent syllables. And there
is a change in attitude too. The introduction had pointed
to the negative aspects of the decay of civilization: it has
no physical vitality, no sap; no vitality of memory, no
tradition; no real freedom. Its positive aspects are simply:

Rocks, moss, stonecrop, iron, merds.

There is no elaboration of meaning. Each word is heavily weighted with suggestion and implication, and left to do its own proliferating work in the reader's mind.

Never, indeed, have words been used in lyric poetry with such insistence on their functional rather than their decorative or musical values—partly, no doubt, because that exuberance of spirits, that press of emotion which seems to demand a rich abundance of expression, is not characteristic of contemporary poets. There are few who 'look upon fine phrases as a lover.' Occasionally we feel that Pegasus is 'dancing with the morning on his flanks,' or has bolted into the air; but in general he is ridden on a tight rein and not given his head.

§

This emphasis on the control of the medium, and the exploitation of it to the utmost, appears in many different ways. During the early years of the twentieth century, poetry in England and America tended to be soft, vague and sentimental. The absence of any fresh vision, and the unresponsiveness to contemporary pressures, held poetic expression at the pastime level, pleasant, harmless and unimportant. The influence of the Imagists imported some definite ideals, which had a tonic effect on versification. Their insistence on the direct treatment of material, and on the utmost economy of presentation, encouraged a new sharpness and sensitiveness of vision and a new discipline of craftsmanship. Poetry dwindled into the keen

visual image and the apt epithet. When William Carlos
Williams describes the coming of spring as

> The alphabet of
> the trees
>
> is fading in the
> song of the leaves

or Wallace Stevens says

> Sombre as fir-trees liquid cats
> Moved in the grass without a sound,

it is the Imagist influence at work. The Sitwells advocated
the vocabulary of interchangeable sense impressions already explored by Rimbaud:

Where the language of one sense is insufficient to cover a
meaning, we use another, and by this means, we attempt
to pierce down to the essence of the thing seen, producing
or heightening its significance by discovering in it attributes which at first sight seem alien, but which are actually related.

Pushed to its extreme, this resulted in Edith Sitwell's writing of a 'Martha-coloured scabious,' because she had once
had a nurse called Martha who wore a scabious-colored
dress. But we may find a fastidious example of this practice
in Dylan Thomas,

These once blind eyes have breathed a wind of vision,

and it appears more acrobatically in E. E. Cummings:

my mind is
a big chunk of irrevocable nothing which touch &
taste & smell & hearing & sight keep hitting &
chipping with sharp fatal tools
in an agony of sensual chisels i perform squirms of

chrome & execute strides of cobalt
nevertheless i
feel that i cleverly am being altered that i slightly am
myself
Hereupon helpless i utter lilac shrieks and scarlet
bellowings.

But as Whitehead says, 'Sense perception, despite its
prominence in consciousness, belongs to the superficiali-
ties of experience,' and the new awareness of the subtleties
of the poetic medium goes a good deal further than descriptive economy. It involves not only a new vividness,
but a new intensification in the use of language. From the
Metaphysicals the moderns learned to juxtapose and fuse
different qualities of experience and vocabulary, the abstract emotion or idea and the concrete sense impression.
When Crane speaks shudderingly of love as 'a burnt match
skating in a urinal,' or Cummings writes 'the great black
preacher gargles jesus,' or Eberhart 'the five hates of a
claw,' the words of each phrase convey both a vivid visual
image and a particular emotional coloring and implication which can afford to dispense with any logical statement or further definition. They are illustrations in brief
of the logic of the imagination.

Like the Metaphysicals, too, the moderns will fuse passion and verbal wit to gain emotional or satiric effects.
When Eliot writes,

I journeyed to the timekept City,
Where the River flows, with foreign flotations,

the play on words emphasizes his irony of vision. 'Timekept' implies both the idea of the ubiquitous church
chimes, bells reminiscent of centuries of tradition, and of

the innumerable lives in the business quarter of London, 'the City,' which are regulated by inflexible 'office hours'; while in the second line the whole idea of modern financial civilization and 'big business' is telescoped with the idea of the part the River has played in all the past history of the city.

§

A further illustration of the poet's increased sensitiveness to word value is seen in the enormous enlargement of his potential vocabulary. Both the eighteenth and the nineteenth centuries regarded poetry as speech dressed in its Sunday best. The poet's tongue was not only language heightened by rhythm, meter and concentration; it was a *different* language from that of common speech, a language with a strong tinge of snobbery in it, which could not mix with the vulgar tongue. The critic who declared that the word 'bloated' could not appear in poetry, because it was sacred to the description of dead fish, illustrates the attitude. But the moderns will have none of such limitations, and if we take any piece of good verse of the present day it is obvious at once that it is based on the common idiom of educated people, as in *Portrait* by Robert Fitzgerald:

> *Who doubts the fitting key*
> *Who serves another's eye*
> *Whose hand is not his own*
> *Who never thought he won*
>
> *Who watches the leaf turn*
> *When the rose child is born*
> *Who hears the mouth of death*
> *Repeat a dry myth*

The brutal present and the soft past
His constants are; all else is variable;
Through waking weather and its climates of dream
That mathematic shapes his character;

As one love-lost, bemused by memory,
He smiles, moves sunny hands, goes out
To April's fairest air or to machine guns
Punching in dust their rows of periods.

The tone is free from strain or decoration, and this flavor of direct speech, as we have already seen in the discussion of pattern, is by far the most popular mode of our age. Pound remains the greatest artist in its felicitous handling. He did not, of course, invent the form. Clough wrote verse in that style some ninety years ago:

Dulce it is, and *decorum*, no doubt for the country to fall, to
Offer one's blood an oblation to Freedom, and die for the Cause; yet
Still, individual culture is also something. . . .

The ground was further broken by Browning. When Pound opens a poem:

Damn it all! all this our South stinks peace.
You whoreson dog, Papiols, come! Let's to music!
I have no life save when the swords clash,

it is easy to see from whom he has borrowed that manner of seizing the situation by the scruff of its neck, and startling the reader by his colloquial energy. But it was the French poet Laforgue who taught Pound and Eliot their subtle conversational tone, and the mixture of vocabularies in a single poem, which particularly influenced Eliot. The influence of Laforgue was purely literary, and

it is a strange anomaly that the age which has so emphasized the importance of the common word in poetry
has produced poetry so remote from the common life.

§

Besides the use of the speech idiom and the bare word,
there is the further addition in modern usage of the direct
colloquialism and of slang. Here too there is a debt to
Browning, whom the moderns habitually underrate as an
artist, presumably because of his 'Hurrah for the Universe'
spirit. And it is true that the moderns often use the trick
with much more subtlety than Browning. Auden is especially skillful in merging the slangy and the pure word
so that they reinforce one another:

Lawrence, Blake and Homer Lane, once healers in our
    land;
These are dead as iron for ever; these can never hold our
    hand.

Lawrence was brought down by smut-hounds, Blake went
    dotty as he sang. . . .

And Yeats has the great craftsman's ability to make any
kind of word pliable to his purpose, putting a racy concrete colloquialism in the midst of an abstract argument
without any incongruity:

> I mock Plotinus' thought
> And cry in Plato's teeth,
> Death and life were not
> Till man made up the whole,
> Made lock, stock and barrel
> Out of his bitter soul.

Pound gains a similar widening effect by his juxtaposition of traditional and contemporary vocabulary in his *Homage to Sextus Propertius:*

> My cellar does not date from Numa Pompilius,
> Nor bristle with wine jars,
> Nor is it equipped with a frigidaire patent. . . .

Here the value of the modern usage springs directly from incongruity. The poet Propertius conveys in this group of images the fact that he is a poor man lacking the luxuries which betoken taste and wealth. But Pound, by his introduction of the contrast between vintage cellars and the refrigerator, establishes not only the quality of the civilization in which Propertius wrote his songs, but compares that civilization with the contemporary world.

§

Another stratagem of language peculiar to present-day poets is their use of quotation and allusion. Influences and imitation of earlier writers can always be traced in poets. Eberhart will sound like Donne:

> Yet when we loved we thought we changed,
> Each each other's self became,
> Thus hardly from the first had ranged
> And wore Love's, the third, his name.

Or Day Lewis will sound like Hopkins:

> Where's that unique one, wind and wing married,
> Aloft in contact of earth and ether,
> Feathery my comet. Oh too often
> From heaven harried by carrion cares.

While Eliot's echo is to be met everywhere, an embarrassing parrot,

rejoicing
at nothing, or rejoicing that one can so rejoice
at nothing,

or declaring that 'the spider weaves over tomorrow,' or 'we fought at the dikes in the bright sun,' or crying 'Where are the lighthouses and the beacons?'

But the deliberate technical use of borrowed material is quite different from this, and is made to serve many purposes by the poets who use it—notably Pound, Eliot and Marianne Moore. Pound's extravagant use of erudition has already been discussed. Too frequently he lays on learning with a trowel, smothering his poetic substance instead of fertilizing it. It is in his capacity for assimilating quotation and allusion into his own personal rhythm and vision that Eliot is so much more skillful than Pound. It is true that the demands which Eliot makes on his reader's literary equipment hinder the communication of his full content, but even without knowledge of his sources *something* comes through, in the way of tone or rhythm, whereas Pound's chunks of Provençal, Italian, Latin and Greek will often block all communication.

Edmund Wilson has estimated that in *The Waste Land* there are quotations and allusions from about thirty-five different writers. This illustrates how essential to Eliot's technical method is his system of borrowing. It is a deliberate device by which he accomplishes complex effects with great compression and swiftness. These may be effects of ironic contrast, as in *Burbank with a Baedeker: Bleistein with a Cigar*. Here, on the one hand, the disparity between the Venice of the modern tourist, academic or vulgar, and the Venice of noble tradition, and on the other hand, the contrast between heroic loves and coarse promiscuity, are captured, simply by trailing across the reader's sensibility the allusive scent of literary quotation and reference. Or the allusions may suddenly focus a general impression, as when the ominous vague drama in *Sweeney among the Nightingales* takes a deeper significance from the reference to Agamemnon in the last stanza. Or they may be orchestrated into one dominant emotional theme, as in the conclusion of *The Burial of the Dead*, where references to Baudelaire, to Dante's hell and to Webster's *The White Devil* blend with hallucinations and memories to create a sense of the living death in the 'Unreal City.' A further general effect gained by this device of multiplied allusion in *The Waste Land* is to emphasize the poet's awareness of the disintegration of modern civilization, the fact that it is 'a heap of broken images.' By drawing upon such a diversity of material from the past, by amassing such a heap of broken cultures, he implies the absence of any central and stable artistic and intellectual reality.

The poetry of Marianne Moore, even more than that of Pound and Eliot, is a mosaic of acknowledged quotation, but her borrowings only remotely resemble theirs. She does not seek to expand her implications nor to exploit atmosphere and reminiscence by her allusiveness. The source of her quotation rarely has any relation to its effect. It is the substance of the quotation itself which is functional—as metaphor, as statement or as idea: it is an elaborately contrived *mot juste*. A typical instance occurs in *Novices:*

Acquiring at thirty what at sixty they will be trying to
    forget,
blind to the right word, deaf to satire
which like 'the smell of the cypress strengthens the nerves
    of the brain,'
averse from the antique
with 'that tinge of sadness about it which a reflective mind
    always feels,
it is so little and so much'—
they write the sort of thing that would in their judgment
    interest a lady. . . .

Neither of these quotations is exact, each has been altered
to suit the required structural rhythm: nor is it of the
least consequence that one is from Landor and the other
from the notice of a sale of Chinese objects of art in *The
Illustrated London News*. They are simply an illustration
and a remark which the poet found already phrased to
suit her purpose. Having found it, she took a craftsman's
delight in fitting it into her rhythmical scheme. It is a
comment both on Marianne Moore's genius in adapting
material, and on the adaptable and neighborly nature of
words, that quotations from such a variety of sources
can be so happily accommodated within poetry of such
restrained pitch.

CHAPTER 12

The Poet and the Community

No art can conquer the people alone—the people
are conquered by an ideal of life held up by authority. As this ideal is rediscovered, the arts, music and
poetry, painting and literature, will draw closer
together.

w. b. yeats. *Dramatis Personae*

POETRY can never be a 'pure' art in the sense that
music is. Its medium is language, and language,
besides being the medium of poetry, is the medium
of all general communication between human beings.
Hence poetry is indissolubly alloyed with the matter of
life. No one expects music—except martial and such music
—to have a social 'use': it functions as aesthetic experience
and as entertainment. But there is a never-ending argument between poets and the public, and among poets
themselves, as to what their function in the community
is, and how they should achieve it. The poet is a specially
sensitive individual, says one school of thought; he is in
society but not of it; he can only be fully himself by
ignoring the public; he is by nature an anarchic individualist; his sole function is to seek truth and to master his
craft; he is self-sufficient, his world is within himself; his
work exists only on the plane of 'significant form.' You
do not ask Keats' Grecian Urn to hold water, or Shelley's
West Wind to grind corn. The other school replies: The
poet cannot divorce himself from society. He has always

had a social function, 'to lift the hearts and soothe the cares of men'; it is true that he is more complex and sensitive than his fellows, but basically he shares their common humanity, and his gifts enable him to reveal the ordinary man to himself, and to enlarge his scope, by expressing in words what his less gifted fellows dumbly feel; moreover, he needs the assurance that he has this function in human society, and he must, if necessary, compromise with his individualist impulses to achieve it. 'Poetry,' says Louis MacNeice, 'should steer a middle course between pure entertainment and propaganda.'

Meanwhile the poor Muse must be a little bewildered: almost as bewildered as God in the last war:

> God heard the embattled nations sing and shout:
> *Gott Strafe England* and *God save the King*,
> God this, God that, and God the other thing.
> 'Good God' said God, 'I've got my work cut out.'

§

There are certain things about poets which apply in all ages, and which perhaps the disgruntled modern poet is apt to forget. One is that they are no different from ordinary mortals in craving for an harmonious and abundant life, and in liking to feel that they are of some value to the community. Another is that though their audience may be specially restricted today, poets, with a few lucky exceptions, have never had assured positions in society. We have only to read of the lives of the Elizabethan dramatists, of the scramble for patronage in the eighteenth century, of the poverty of the romantics, to realize how precarious and how misprized a calling poetry has always been.

> Seven wealthy towns contend for Homer dead
> Through which the living Homer begged his bread.

But that the living poet has been more often than not disparaged by all but a very small section of the public does not discredit the poet's instinct that he is of supreme value to the community, nor prove that his concern about the position of his art in modern society is unjustified.

The extreme self-consciousness of the poet today, with his anxiety to define his function, is a symptom of this condition. The poet is no longer taken for granted. In earlier days, however much the individual poet was neglected, the value of poetry itself was never questioned by society. Nowadays it is. Apart from the extreme position of those who feel that all art is irrelevant at the moment, and had better go into cold storage until matters such as the class war, economic chaos and political dictatorship have been settled, there is the general position that poetry is not read by people whose main interests lie in other forms of intelligent activity. Public men of today are seldom educated in literature as our ancestors were, hence political action is no longer linked with cultural tradition. Among 'the people,' mechanized amusements have swamped reading, and the singing or reciting of popular verse. Poetry is obviously no longer a part of their national and natural life. Industrial civilization changed the poet's world, and poets, both great and small, found it impossible to come to terms with it. Their poetry was a poetry of protest. Yeats withdrew to a lonely aristocratic grandeur, or made symbols of his own wisdom, lust and anger in the figures of simple peasants; Lawrence withdrew from the poverty and ugliness of his own working class to a primitive source of energy; Pound from his own country to a purely personal culture; Eliot to a spiritual discipline; the Surrealists into the world of the subconscious. Shorn of her traditional audience, poetry broke with her own traditions and adopted isms instead, emphasizing 'form' out of all proportion to 'content.' From its position as a universal activity, it fell to that of a technical branch of culture. It deliberately contracted itself in an effort to isolate its quintessential quality. It drew its skirts away from the contamination of religion, philosophy, ethics, politics or entertainment, and followed the trend of the times into a rigid specialization of its own departmental technique. It could find no common ground on which it might meet intelligent men in other walks of life. Revolted by the ugliness of the society with which it was invited to mate, it weakened its stock with inbreeding and spiritual incest. For as Eliot says, 'If you aim only at the poetry in poetry there is no poetry.'

§

Something of this sort has always happened in times of social unrest. The present age has instinctively turned to the seventeenth century, an age of civil disturbance and changing culture. In that century too poetry found itself cut off from a vital relationship with the public life of the time, and turned in upon its own technical problems, absorbed in the subjective response of the individual to experience rather than in any objective vision of universal values.

This is the complaint which is constantly brought against the present age, and it is just, since it is true. But it is hardly fair to blame it on the poets. The fact that we are all, as Arnold felt,

> Wandering between two worlds, one dead
> The other powerless to be born,

that we are all alive at a time when a past culture is dying and a new one has not yet declared itself, is not the fault of the poets. In great creative ages society absorbs ideas easily from its men of genius and uses them as a source of spiritual nourishment. At such times it seems as if the level of general humanity in the men of genius is particularly high; they emphasize in their work the permanent elements in human life which unite all men. The man of genius and the ordinary citizen seem to speak the same language. And at such times there is always a great deal of narrative or dramatic poetry at the level of the common logical use of language—as exemplified nowadays in the poetry of Robert Frost. There is a feeling in such poetry that the artist values his art primarily as a means of communicating the values he discerns in life. He is *primarily* concerned with art as a medium in which to create life; he is not *primarily* concerned with the technical problems of language as a medium in which to create art. It is a matter of where the emphasis falls. And the values he discerns in life are large, simple moral and emotional principles which hold a united society together as the principle of gravity holds the solar system in operation. At such times there appears to be no conflict between the artist and his environment. Poets such as Chaucer and Browning are instances of such artists.

In less well-integrated ages, when a culture is beginning to decay, the great artist will, like Milton and Words-worth, protest against its degeneration, affirming his own principles, but feeling himself in revolt from his environment. Finally, when the culture is dying, and the principles set up by its men of genius in the past appear to have exhausted their vitality, the men of genius themselves lose their integration. Tortured by the conflict between themselves and society, they are conscious of a spiritual exile. In such circumstances the poet can achieve harmony by the artistic interpretation of his own response to the state of disintegration, creating another mode of life from his own death, like Kafka, or Eliot in *The Waste Land* or most of the minor poets of today.

§

Poetry is consciously created, but a culture cannot be consciously created. It is the soil of a society's life, the source of its homogeneity, and it cannot be enriched by art unless that art is in a form which the culture can assimilate. Hence the sense of rootlessness of the modern poet, and the conviction that he can communicate with only a few of his fellows. This was, perhaps, the situation of the seventeenth century poets, but it mattered less to them, since the 'areas of sensibility' they were interested in exploring were those of religion and love, which belong to the private and personal aspects of human experience. But the situation is aggravated for the modern poet since one subject which interests him deeply is the relation of the individual to the community. Almost all the young poets of today long to establish themselves as a living part of society, and feel frustrated because society can receive nothing that they can give:

We are left alone with our day and the time is short and
        History to the defeated
May say Alas but cannot help nor pardon.*

Because poetry has no congenial social environment from which to draw nourishment, or which it can nourish, any affirmative poetry of our age has been faced with a choice of alternatives. It could draw its strength from the primitive sources of all life, as Lawrence did, or elaborate, through the intellect and emotions, a personal mythology, as Yeats and Eliot did. It is significant that both these writers are distinguished critics as well as poets.

§

The lesser poets are not doomed to silence. There are no conditions in which poets are doomed to silence. But they become increasingly tormented by a sense of living unfulfillment and choked activity. This does not mean that the present age has not produced distinguished poetry, for it has. If we come to our poetry on the lookout only for things which are not there, we shall omit to notice the things which are there. The poetry of today may not possess the qualities of poetry of another day, but this does not mean that it is not poetry. In subject matter we must not forget the uncovering of regions of the mind hitherto unexplored. And in form, the technical experimentation of the poets of the last twenty years points to

* W. H. Auden. *Spain.*

the life which is in the poetic tradition, and not to its death. But it is true that the vitality of poetry has been driven inwards instead of spreading outwards, and poets have inclined to regard 'the poetry in poetry' as its supreme significance:

> The great division in all—I mean *all* contemporary writers—is between that little that has been written by men who 'clarified their intention'; who were writing with the *sole aim* of registering and communicating truth or their desire, and the overwhelming bulk composed of the consciously dishonest *and* of those whose writing has been affected at second or tenth remove by economic pressure, economic temptation, economic flattery. . . .

This would sound plausible, if we did not at once remember the great quantity of first-rate literary work in the past, from the plays of Shakespeare downwards, produced in the way of popular commercial commissions to give the public the entertainment it wanted, or produced by artists who adjusted their personal expression towards extending the social availability of their work.

There are always poets who write with 'the sole aim of registering and communicating truth or their desire.' Among such poets in the present day we might instance Dylan Thomas. But there are other poets whose work acknowledges a dependence on their environment. Artists are sometimes regarded as maintaining a position implicit in the old joke of the newspaper headlines, 'Fog in the English Channel: the Continent Isolated'; but most poets today are fully alive to the fact that it is the poet, and not the bulk of mankind, who is now in the position of isolation. Since therefore it is the instinct of the poet, in common with most other men, to feel himself an essential part of society, he is driven to take action about his present situation. And he may do this in a variety of ways.

Political and economic order is the external order of society, and though the poet may identify himself with propaganda on its behalf it is not, for him, the essential order. The poet's essential order comprehends the whole nature of man. This he interprets through the art of patterned language. Looked at from this point of view, the most obscure Surrealist poem is an attempt to objectify an aspect of human truth, even if it is the elusive truth of the subconscious. At the other extreme is the wider focus advocated by Louis MacNeice:

I would have the poet able-bodied, fond of talking, a reader of the newspapers, capable of pity and laughter, informed in economics, appreciative of women, involved in personal relationships, actively interested in politics, susceptible to physical impressions.

This is the ideal behind the type of verse which Cyril Connolly aptly describes as 'an affable verbal newsreel.' Between these extremes lies the bulk of modern poetry.

Much of this poetry is an integration of the prevailing mood of disintegration, an harmonious expression of the state of disharmony. It *creates* the truth of the situation, without explicit comment. It reveals; it does not interpret. Its power of communication lies not in lucidity but in intensity.

Creative power is of many different kinds, but the two elements in it which operate with the greatest force are *intensity* and *intelligence*. The former is the quintessence of poetic genius, and operates in its most concentrated form in lyric poetry; the latter, a no less vital source of energy, is the element of the common man in the poet, and the strongest link between himself and society. It is a comprehensive quality. It is the element which Eliot emphasizes when he says that the struggle of our time is 'to renew our association with traditional wisdom; to re-establish a vital connection between the individual and the race,' and it includes also what Auden means when he says 'in literature I expect plenty of news.'

§

One considerable step towards the creation of a contemporary poetry which unites intensity with intelligence has been accomplished by the poetic medium developed in the past twenty years. The use of the English language in poetry has been revolutionized. The poets have fashioned speech rhythms and the idiom of everyday into the instrument of verse. Chesterton said of Browning that 'he substituted the blue spurt of a lighted match for the monotony of the evening star,' and indeed Browning, like Whitman, was a great pioneer in the enfranchisement of words. 'Poetic diction' no longer rules poetry. Today the poetic vocabulary can be as impassioned as *Gerontion*, as graceful and ceremonious as Pound's *Cathay*, as easily familiar as Auden's *Voltaire at Ferney*. It can accommodate rhetoric and hyperbole, political and scientific jargon, colloquialism and slang. It is the poetic idiom of a democratic age.

But we are left with the question whether the poet, even if he possesses a democratic idiom, can speak in any universal way to a society which has so little common basis of understanding. Can he say anything of 'social significance,' can he help to build and sustain any social structure, until a social structure is built which can sustain him?

§

It has been said that a civilization is revealed by its myths. We live by spiritual, intellectual, moral and physical values, and these are incarnate to us in the popular stories and figures which are the outward symbols of the instinct, wisdom and intelligence of the race. They do not embody aspects of reality which exist only for a specially equipped audience, as do the personal phantasmagorias of *The Waste Land* and *Ulysses,* which are the literary myths of our own day. The popular myth exists for everybody; it is planted in the common ground which the artist shares with the public. In all creative ages, such as the fifth century B. C. or the Elizabethan or Victorian age in England, popular literature of the period is full of popular fables and figures—social myths, which embody the culture of the age and universalize common human experience. Now, in addition to the poverty of fresh symbols, the people have lost their vital connection with the past. The classical mythologies, the heroes of romance, the stories of the Bible and the Christian ethic, no longer unite all classes in a community of understanding. These traditions and the thought behind them are no longer a common cultural heritage; and we have no contemporary storehouse such as was provided by the Elizabethan drama or the Victorian novel. We have Ferdinand the Bull, Mickey Mouse and the comic strips. But if literature is to play its part in a revitalization of society, it can only be by the revitalization of such traditional symbols or by the creation of new ones embodying the living values in our own society.

This cannot be done by books *about* things, by what we might call 'applied' literature. Nowadays there is a host of such books: books *about* how to live and make friends, about current concrete interests, about politics, economics, sociology, psychology, internationalism or education. Perhaps it is natural, since society is engaged in such immediate and concrete struggles, that the literature of knowledge should usurp the place of the literature of power in this way; but the loss to the community is incalculable. For the scope of creative art is infinitely more comprehensive and vital than that of analysis. One incarnates the values we live by, the other criticizes them; one reveals them, the other explains them. It is the difference between a living body and a lecture on biology.

§

The only effort to achieve a 'social' poetry fusing intensity and intelligence in a direct portrayal of life has been in the attempt to popularize the poetic drama. But drama must be dramatic, and the poet cannot compass dramatic imagination to order. First-rate descriptive and analytic verse, such as the choruses in *The Dog beneath the Skin*, or the brilliant doggerel-dialogue in the same play, is not enough; nor is the quite sincere political feeling behind MacLeish's *Panic* or Spender's *Trial of a Judge*. Drama is the representation of human life in terms of character and action. Fables and figures universalizing common human experience are essential to a popular drama: without these it cannot live. Eliot's *Murder in the Cathedral* was interesting in its effort to appeal at different *levels* of understanding, in the same way as Shakespeare's plays do: to achieve a synthesis of intensity and intelligence by the combining of a fable, intelligible to all, with the choruses which projected the action in terms of the poetic logic of symbol, image and rhythm. And Auden's *The Ascent of F6* attempted a different synthesis in which a psychological study of a sensitive individual should be seen against the background of the external social forces which inevitably wreck him. But Eliot's play, for all its formal beauty, never realized itself in terms of flesh and blood, and Auden's conception never emerged into clear-cut form, but remained blurred and muddled.

We come back, then, to the question, What can the poet do at a time when external struggles for power consume the energies of nations and classes, when disillusionment debilitates the spirit of man, and when a crude social culture saps the soul of the people? If, as I. A. Richards says, 'Art is the point at which the growth of the mind reveals itself,' it appears as if the point has not yet been reached when the society of the future will be heralded by a new revolutionary poet. There is no one now writing who points authoritatively in a new direction in the way in which Eliot, Pound and D. H. Lawrence did twenty years ago. But there are persistent *attempts* now to make poetry functional in society instead of a decoration upon it, just as there are persistent and inextinguishable attempts to reorganize society itself.

What form of synthesis will emerge from the present state of crisis in either it is naturally impossible to foretell. If the basis for any widely diffused culture of the future is the economic security of the individual, we may hope for a real proletarian literature, no longer on the barren theme of the proletarian as the underdog. It will portray the proletarian not as the helpless victim of economic exploitation, but as a man, rejoicing in his humanity. It will create myths of man's heroic virtues, though maybe it will use the most material, humble, particular and topical stories and symbols as their background. Nor need it be written by members of the proletariat. Creative genius is no respecter of class. Even Marx, much as he disliked Tolstoi, was forced to own that no one had succeeded in creating a genuine Russian peasant in literature 'until this Count came on the scene.' The only essential of such a future literature is that it will incorporate a fundamental concurrence about the universal values of life, shared by both society and the writer. The poet's function, as it has always been, will be to deepen the reality of those values and to widen their scope. But meanwhile, bourgeois and workers who both envisage a future unified society have a long way to go. The left-wing poet, unless he possesses the creative genius of a Tolstoi, is apt to find himself in a world where his intellectual sympathies are with one class while his whole social consciousness still belongs to the other. His condition is further complicated by an acute awareness of his 'selfhood' which has rendered him supersensitive to his own malady. At the other end the workers, having lost all their old cultural traditions, and having nothing at present to take their place, produce no popular art.

'If a great change is to be made in human affairs, the

minds of men will be fitted to it; the general opinions and feelings will draw that way,' said Edmund Burke; and that must be the basis of any evolution or revolution. We are in an era when poetry's organic function in the fabric of civilization has been lost, and it will not be regained until that fabric is repaired or refashioned. But the poet remains, as always, one of the potential instruments to that end. He keeps our sensibilities alive, and in the midst of the present chaos of violence, greed and dirt he is

The voice of Man: 'O teach me to outgrow my madness:
Ruffle the perfect manners of the frozen heart,
And once again compel it to be awkward and alive,
To all it suffered once a weeping witness.
Clear from the head the masses of impressive rubbish;
Rally the lost and trembling forces of the will,
Gather them up and let them loose upon the earth,
Till they construct at last a human justice,
The contribution of our star, within the shadow
Of which uplifting, loving, and constraining power
All other reasons may rejoice and operate.' *

* W. H. Auden.

Index